SAMUEL TAKES A BREAK...
IN MALE DUNGEON NO. 5
AFTER A LONG BUT
GENERALLY SUCCESSFUL
DAY OF TOURS

by Rhianna Ilube

Samuel Takes a Break was first performed at The Yard Theatre, London, on 9 February 2024.

SAMUEL TAKES A BREAK

by Rhianna Ilube

CAST
Bola Akeju | Orange
Fode Simbo | Samuel
Stefan Asante-Boateng | Trev
Tori Allen-Martin | Letty

CREATIVE AND PRODUCTION TEAM
Rhianna Ilube | Writer
Anthony Simpson-Pike | Director
Milla Clarke | Set and Costume Designer
XANA | Sound Designer
Christopher Nairne | Lighting Designer
Gino Ricardo Green | Video Designer
Sung Im Her | Movement Director
Jatinder Chera | Casting Director
Taiwo Ava Oyebola | Assistant Director
Joel Trill | Voice Coach
Esi Acquaah | Associate Voice Coach
Jacob Roberts-Mensah | Cultural Consultant
James Dawson | Production Manager
Wabriya King | Production Dramatherapist
Male Arcucci | Costume Supervisor
Aïsha Kent | Company Stage Manager
Africa Blagrove | Assistant Stage Manager

BIOGRAPHIES

Bola Akeju

Bola Akeju plays Orange. Bola has just finished leading in *School Girls; or, The African Mean Girls Play* at the Lyric Hammersmith, earning a nomination for a Black British Theatre Award for her role. She recently played opposite Bukky Bakray in *The Girls' Club* and features in the third season of Jason Sudeikis's Emmy Award-winning series *Ted Lasso*. Bola left RADA early to play the lead in *Klippies* at the Young Vic.

Fode Simbo

Fode Simbo plays Samuel. He graduated from the Guildhall School of Music and Drama, and gained recognition for his role as Samuel in *Under the Kunde Tree* at Southwark Playhouse, earning a nomination for Best Supporting Actor at the Black British Theatre Awards.

His stage credits for The Yard Theatre include Dipo Baruwa-Etti's *An unfinished man*. Other recent stage credits include *Macbeth* (Shakespeare's Globe); *Young Marx* (The Bridge Theatre) and *SOLARIS* (Lyric Hammersmith/Edinburgh Lyceum). His TV credits include *The Reckoning*, *Vigil*, *Summer of Rockets*, *Little Women* (BBC); *Andor* (Disney+); *Hijack* (Apple TV); and *Philip K Dick: Electric Dreams* (Channel 4). His film credits include *Fisherman's Friends* (Fred Films).

Stefan Asante-Boateng

Stefan Asante-Boateng plays Trev. He is a British actor of Ghanaian heritage and has been acting for over ten years. He trained at the Identity School of Acting.

His most recent screen credits include playing CPS Judge Kwame Boateng on ITV's long-running soap *Coronation Street*; BBC's *Killing Eve*; R.M Moses' *Grounding* and Moderator TV mini-series *Suffering*, directed and written by Sinitta Monero. Stage credits include *Brit Aint Right* (Maktub Theatre); *Eggs In The Basket* (Courtyard Theatre); *Choices* (tour) and *Dancing and Drumming to Doom* (Ujaama Arts). He appeared in the feature film *The Fallout* and the short films *Tina* and *Meaning* (Inner Eye Productions); *It Takes A Town* (Ebonics Films); *Meet Me By The Sea*, *The Moderator*, *At Play* (Your Cinema Films) *Grounding* (Blame The Consumer); *Red Flag* (Nort3y Productions); *The Other Side* and *2 Bags* (Red Stream Media).

In 2020, he won a Screen Nation Award for Best Actor in a Series for his work on the TV mini-series *Suffering*.

Tori Allen-Martin

Tori Allen-Martin plays Letty. Tori is a regular in BBC 1 comedy *Here We Go* alongside Katherine Parkinson and Alison Steadman and was previously seen as a leading regular in four series of BBC's *London Kills* and as a regular on Channel 4's *Pure.*

On stage, Tori has appeared in *Park Bench* (Park Theatre); *One Man, Two Guvnors* (New Wolsey, Ipswich/Nuffield Southampton); *The Hardest One* (The Other Place/Criterion); *Boxed* (Made in LDN Collective); *Wretch* (Vaults Festival) and *Streets* (Hackney Empire). Her work in musicals includes *Then, Now and Next* (Southwark Playhouse); *The Season* (Glass Half Full Productions and Tim Johanson); *Rock of Ages* (DLAP Entertainment); *Muted* (Interval Productions); *H.R.Hairth* (Iris Theatre); *Yarico* (John and Jodie Kidd and Crow and Elk); *Rent* (Interval Productions); *Hair – Help for Heroes* (Piccadilly Theatre); *After the Turn* (My Protegee with Interval Productions); *Hair the Musical* (European tour); *Hair* (arena tour Holland). On television she has appeared in *Mrs Sidhu Investigates* (Acorn); *Significant Other* (Hatrick); *Plebs: The War (the finale)* (Rise Films); *The Other Half* (Ranga Bee Productions); *Flatshare* (42 for Paramount+); *Here We Go, Pandemonium* (BBC); *London Kills* (Acorn); and *Back To Life* (Two Brothers Pictures). Other performances include *First Things Last: Lance Horne* (Lincoln Centre NYC/Spekulation Entertainment); *Higher – Eliza and the Bear* (recording); *The Road Less Travelled – The Take Movie Soundtrack* (recording); and *Christmas in New York* (Manchester Palace/Palace West End).

Rhianna Ilube

Rhianna Ilube is a playwright and event curator from London. Her debut play, *Samuel Takes a Break*, was Highly Commended for the Soho Theatre's Verity Bargate Award, and shortlisted for the Women's Prize for Playwriting. She is a member of the Soho Six and an alumni of the Royal Court Intro Group, the Oxford Playmakers, and BBC London Voices. Rhianna was previously Associate Director at Coney, where she co-created and wrote *1884*, a new immersive game-theatre show premiering in spring 2024. She is a film programmer for BFI Flare and has produced events for cultural venues and NGOs across London and Berlin since 2015.

Anthony Simpson-Pike

Anthony Simpson-Pike is a director, dramaturg and writer. He is currently Deputy Artistic Director at The Yard Theatre and was previously Associate Director at the Gate Theatre. Anthony is also a facilitator, having worked with young people and communities at the Gate, the Royal Court, the Young Vic, the Globe, and the National Theatre. Recent directorial work includes the Olivier Award-winning *The P Word* and *Lava* at the Bush; *An Octoroon* at the Abbey, Dublin; *Living Newspaper* at the Royal Court; *The Electric* for Paines Plough and the Royal Welsh College of Music and Drama; and *The Ridiculous Darkness* at the Gate, London.

As a dramaturg, Anthony has developed multiple seasons of work for the Gate and The Yard. Recent dramaturgical credits include: *Much Ado About Nothing* for the RSC; *Samskara* at The Yard Theatre; *Hotline* with Produced Moon at the Tron; *Dear Young Monster* by Pete McHale for The Queer House; and *Coup de Grâce* at the Royal Court. *Samuel Takes a Break* will be the first play Anthony has directed at The Yard Theatre.

Milla Clarke

Milla was the winner of the Linbury Prize for Stage Design in 2015. Other awards include the Lord Williams Prize for Design and The Prince of Wales Design Scholarship

Designs include: *Mates in Chelsea, Inside Bitch, Bad Roads B, Human Animals* (Royal Court); *Cat On A Hot Tin Roof* (Royal Exchange); *Macbeth* (The Reykjavik City Theatre in Iceland); *Bootycandy, A Small Place* (Gate Theatre, London); *Shooting Hedda Gabler* (costumes for Rose Theatre); *Red Ellen* (Northern Stage); *Ivy Tiller: Vicar's Daughter, Squirrel Killer* and *O, Island!* (Mischief Festival for Royal Shakespeare Company); *Isla* (Theatr Clwyd); *La Traviata* (Nevill Holt); *La bohème* (costumes for ENO: Drive & Live); *The Brief and Frightening Reign of Phil* (co-designed with Chloe Lamford for The New Zealand Festival Theatre); *Yolk and Aliens* (co-created with Jane Horrocks, Molly Vivian and Francesca Levi for Brighton Festival); *Curious* (co-designed with Rosie Elnile for Soho Theatre); *Mr Burns* and *Gone Too Far* (Guildhall); *There Are No Beginnings* (Leeds Playhouse); *A Midsummer Night's Dream* (National Youth Theatre); *Europe, You Got Older* (LAMDA); *Beginners* (Unicorn Theatre); *Elephant* (Birmingham Rep); *Outside, Out of Water* (Orange Tree Theatre); *The Tide Whisperer* (National Theatre Wales); *Highway One* (August 012/Wales Millennium Centre); *Frogman* (Curious Directive/ Traverse Theatre); *Paul Bunyan, The Day After, Trial by Jury* (English National Opera). Other designs include *No Place for a Woman* (Theatre503); *Yuri* (Chapter, Cardiff).

Milla trained at the Royal Welsh College of Music and Drama, graduating with a first-class BA Hons degree in Theatre Design.

XANA

XANA is a freestyle live loop musician, composer, spatial sound artist, and a haptic specialist sound designer developing accessible audio systems for live art spaces. XANA is a music technology lead at sound research label Inventing Waves supporting other artists and inventors. XANA's recent work includes: *The Architect* (ATC/GDIF); *Shifters, Elephant* (Bush Theatre); *Imposter 22* (Royal Court); *Earthworks, Sundown Kiki Reloaded* (Young Vic); *The Trials, Marys Seacole* (Donmar Warehouse).

Christopher Nairne

Christopher was a 2023 Offies finalist for *Blackout Songs* (Hampstead Theatre). He was also previously a finalist in 2020 for *Preludes*, and won the award in 2016 for *Teddy* (both Southwark Playhouse). Previous productions at The Yard Theatre include *This Beautiful Future* and *Blue Stockings* (National Youth Theatre).

Other theatre includes: Mischief Theatre's *Groan Ups* (West End/ UK tour); *Boy Parts, Chasing Bono, Tumulus* (Soho Theatre); *Infamous* (Jermyn Street Theatre); *Tom Fool, Mayfly* (Orange Tree Theatre); *Jeeves & Wooster in Perfect Nonsense, The Last Temptation of Boris Johnson* (UK tours); *Suzy Storck* (Gate Theatre/France tour); *Keep on Walking Federico* (UK tour/ Barcelona); *The Legend of Sleepy Hollow, The Beautiful Game, A Little Princess* (The Other Palace); *Jerusalem* (Watermill Theatre); *Speech & Debate, BU21* (Trafalgar Studios); and Complicité's *Lionboy* (world tour).

Opera work includes: *L'Agrippina* (Barber Opera); *Madame Butterfly, Jephtha, Macbeth* (Ilford Arts); *Belshazzar* (Trinity Laban Conservatoire); *Vivienne* (Linbury Studio, ROH); and *La bohème* (OperaUpClose, 2011 Olivier Award winner).

Gino Ricardo Green

Gino Ricardo Green is a director and video/projection designer. He is co-founder of Black Apron Entertainment.

Credits as Video/Projection Designer include: *Tambo & Bones* (Theatre Royal Stratford East); *August in England, Lava* (Bush Theatre); *Othello* (NT, Co-Video Designer); *The Ballad of St John's Carpark* (Icon Theatre); *Treason: The Musical in Concert* (West End); *That is Not Who I Am* (Royal Court Theatre); *Kabul Goes Pop: Music Television Afghanistan* (Brixton House/HighTide); *Edge* (NYT); *Children's Children* (Director of Photography/Editor – ETT); *Beyond The Canon, Poor Connection* (RADA); *Sweat* (Donmar Warehouse/West End); *Passages: A Windrush Celebration* (Black Apron at the Royal Court); *Hashtag Lightie* (Arcola Theatre); *Lightie* (Gate Theatre); and *The Flea* (The Yard Theatre).

Credits as Associate Video/Projection Designer include: *Small Island* (National Theatre); *Get Up Stand Up! The Bob Marley Musical* (West End); and *Be More Chill* (The Other Palace/ West End).

Sung Im Her

Sung Im Her (Seoul, South-Korea) obtained a master's degree in contemporary dance at Hansung University. In 2004, she moved to Brussels, Belgium to study at P.A.R.T.S., the acclaimed contemporary dance school led by Anne Teresa De Keersmaeker.

After graduating in 2006, she started working with Jan Fabre/ Troubleyn, Les ballets C de la B and Needcompany in Belgium.

In parallel Sung Im Her has been creating works of her own, starting with *Philia* (2012), *En-trance* (2013), *Tuning* (2014) and *You Are Okay!* (2016). She moved to London in 2016.

In 2019, she created two new works: *NUTCRUSHER* and *W.A.Y*. Both works were commissioned by the Korean Arts Council and premiered at the renowned ARKO Arts Theater in Seoul. With *NUTCRUSHER* she was elected by the Korean Arts Council as Best Emerging Artist of 2019. *NUTCRUSHER* was also selected for Aerowaves '21 and in 2022 was a part of Horizon showcase, presented during Edinburgh Fringe Festival where she received a five-star review by *The Skinny*. In 2021, her dance piece *W.A.Y* (re-work) premiered at The Place in London and received a four-star review by the *Guardian*.

Last year, Sung Im Her created *Everything Falls Dramatic* for Korean National Contemporary Dance Company and toured in Seoul, Madrid, Brussels, Manchester and London. Sung Im Her received the Dance Artist of the Year in 2022 by the Korean Ministry of Culture and was recently named as one of ten 'stage sensations to watch out for in 2023' by the *Guardian*. In 2023, she was the movement director for *The Flea* (The Yard Theatre).

Jatinder Chera

Jatinder Chera took a position at the National Theatre, following his graduation from the Casting Certificate at the National Film and Television School. Prior to this, he worked as an actor, having trained at Millennium Performing Arts.

For The Yard Theatre, Jatinder cast *The Flea*. Further credits include: Olivier Award-winning *The P Word*, *A Playlist for the Revolution* and *Sleepova* (Bush Theatre); *The Nutcracker* (Bristol Old Vic); *Up Next Gala 2022* (Lyttelton Theatre, NT); and *A Family Business* (Staatstheater Mainz/UK tour).

As Casting Associate at the National Theatre, he worked on *The Father and the Assassin* (Olivier Theatre).

As Casting Assistant at the National Theatre, Jatinder worked on *Othello*, and *Much Ado About Nothing* (Lyttelton Theatre); *Small Island* (Olivier Theatre); and *Trouble in Mind* (Dorfman Theatre).

Taiwo Ava Oyebola

Taiwo Ava Oyebola is an interdisciplinary artist working across theatre, literature and arts and heritage, based in London. Interrogating the world through their lived experiences, centering the voices of historically overlooked communities is the thread that runs throughout their creative practice. Working intuitively, they use the poetic potential of language to explore afro-futurity, intimacy and care. Their writing has been performed at the Almeida Theatre, Theatre503 and with Talawa Theatre Company. Directing credits: *1961* and *The Sexiest Woman in the World* (The North Wall Arts Centre); *Talking Stages* (Pleasance Theatre). Assistant Directing credits: *here, here, here* (dir. Katie Greenall) and *Man is Di Feast* (dir. Rochelle Thomas).

Joel Trill

Joel trained as a Voice Coach at the Royal Central School of Speech and Drama. While training, he was awarded the VASTA Diversity Scholarship. His recent credits include: *A Strange Loop* (Barbican); *Beautiful Thing, Tambo & Bones* (Theatre Royal Stratford East); *Patriots* (Almeida Theatre); *A Number, Baghdad Cafe* (The Old Vic); *Rockets and Blue Lights* (Royal Exchange Theatre); *Trojan Horse* (Battersea Arts Centre); *A Taste of Honey* (Trafalgar Studios); *Master Harold & The Boys* (National Theatre); *Two Trains Runnin* (Royal & Derngate Theatre); *As You Like It* (Queen's Hornchurch); *Red Dust Road* (National Theatre of Scotland); *Strange Fruit* (The Bush Screen): *Mr Loverman, The Crown* (Season 5&6); *Queen Charlotte, Murder is Easy, Call the Midwife* (Series 13), *Riches, Gangs of London* (Season 2); *Renegade Nell, My Name is Leon, Citadel, The Ancestors* and *Queen & Slim.*

Esi Acquaah

Esi trained at Royal Central School of Speech and Drama in London, UK, where she achieved a MA in Voice Studies.

Theatre work as a Voice and Dialect Coach includes: *The House of Shades* by Beth Steel (Almeida Theatre, featuring Anne-Marie Duff, directed by Blanche McIntyre); *Morinho* (Theatre503, directed by Nancy Medina); *Days of Significance* by Roy Williams, *THIRTEEN* (Arts Ed, School of Acting); *High Table* by Temi Wilkey (Bush Theatre directed by Daniel Bailey); the award-winning *Lava* by Benedict Lombe (Bush Theatre, featuring Ronke Adekoluejo, directed by Anthony Simpson-Pike); *Punk Rock* (Theatre Royal Stratford East); *Sex Education* (Series 3) (Netflix); *Start* (Mountview); *Desert Boy, Love and Money* (LAMDA); *Pigeon English* (Bristol School of Acting directed by Nancy Medina); *Stop Kiss* (RADA); *The Importance of Being Earnest* (English Touring Theatre directed by Denzel Westley-Sanderson); *Nine Night* by Natasha Gordon (Leeds Playhouse, directed by Amanda Huxtable); *All Roads* by Roy Williams (directed by Anastasia Osei-Kuffuor) and *Beneatha's Place* (Young Vic, written and directed by Kwame Kwei-Armah).

Her stage performance experiences include an exciting ten-year world tour (2010-2019 inclusive) with Cirque du Soleil's show – *Totem*, in which she was the lead female singer and original cast member. This was preceded by two years as Rafiki in Disney's *The Legend of the Lion King* at Disneyland Resort, Paris. Other singing and stage experiences includes work with Luther Vandross, classical singer Jessye Norman, Michael Ball, Mariah Carey and Sir Tom Jones. Esi is a former member of UK's London Community Gospel Choir. She sings as Diva Aretha in the UK Ultimate Divas tribute to Diana Ross, Aretha Franklin, Whitney Houston and Tina Turner. She made her West End debut as a singer in the top-selling West End show *Derren Brown – SHOWMAN*, December 2022 and more recently appeared at the Borlase Theatre in Marlow, December 2023.

James Dawson

James Dawson is a Freelance Production Manager for Theatre, Opera and Dance. Working across London, nationally and internationally with a passion for touring work, performance art and community projects. Consistently working across a wide range of projects: such as interactive children's play spaces: REPLAY @ Southbank Centre, the co-production with Headlong on *A View from the Bridge*, young and community-based performances at Birmingham Rep (Order & Chaos) and global touring with performer, Marikiscrycrycry; *GONER*. James has worked at/with IF Opera, Young Vic Theatre, Unicorn Theatre, National Youth Theatre, Chichester Festival Theatre and The Yard Theatre.

Wabriya King

Wabriya is a qualified Dramatherapist (Roehampton University); actress (The Oxford School of Drama); creative facilitator and Reiki practitioner. Wabriya combines her experience to support creatives alongside the rehearsal and performance period. Dramatherapy support credits include: *Beautiful Thing, Tambo & Bones* (Theatre Royal Stratford East); *A Strange Loop* (Barbican); *Cowbois, Falkland Sound, The Empress, Julius Caesar* (RSC); *School Girls; Or, The African Mean Girls Play* (Lyric Hammersmith); Matthew Bourne's *Romeo and Juliet* (New Adventures); *Drive Your Plow Over the Bones of the Dead* (Complicité); *Romeo and Juliet, Secret Life of Bees* (Almeida Theatre); *August in England* (Bush Theatre); *For Black Boys Who Have Considered Suicide When The Hue Gets Too Heavy* (New Diorama Theatre/Royal Court/West End); *Blue* (ENO); *Further than the Furthest Thing* (Young Vic); *Family Tree* (Actors Touring Company); *Bootycandy* (Gate Theatre); *Blues for an Alabama Sky* (National Theatre); *Hamilton, Moulin Rouge* (West End).

Film includes: *Empire of Light, Chevalier.*

Male Arcucci
Born and raised in Buenos Aires, Argentina, Malena Arcucci is
a theatre designer and costume supervisor based in London. She
is co-artistic director of Mariana Malena Theatre, a female-led
Latinx company that focused on devise and collaborative theatre
practices.

Design credits include: *When You Pass Over My Tomb* (Arcola
Theatre); *The Wolf, The Duck and The Mouse* (Unicorn Theatre);
Super Chefs (UK tour); *Strangers Like Me* (NT Connect/Hackney
Shed); *The Bit Players* (Southwark Playhouse); *Friday Night Love
Poem* (Zoo Venues); *Point of No Return* (Summerhall); *The Two of
Us* (Theatre Deli); *Playing Latinx* (Camden's People's Theatre);
and various productions in Buenos Aires, Argentina.

Associate Designer credits include: *Falkland Sound* (RSC); *Dear
Elizabeth* (The Gate); *Chiaroscuro* (Bush Theatre); and *Thebes
Land* (Arcola Theatre).

Costume Supervisor credits include: *The Empress* (RSC/Lyric
Hammersmith); *August in England* (Bush Theatre); *Sucker Punch*
(Queen's Theatre); *Bootycandy* (Gate Theatre); *Super High
Resolution* (Soho Theatre); *The Boys are Kissing* (Theatre503);
A Blues for an Alabama Sky (as Assistant, National Theatre);
The Cherry Orchard (The Yard); *Chasing Hares* (Young Vic); *House
of Ife* (Bush Theatre); *Lotus Beauty*, Raya (Hampstead Theatre);
Moreno, Milk and Gall (Theatre503), amongst others.

Aïsha Kent
Aïsha Kent is a Stage Manager and theatre-maker who trained at
Kent University and Rose Bruford. She is passionate about
working on projects that focus on underrepresented voices.
Recent credits include Technical Stage Manger on critically
acclaimed and award-winning *Dreaming and Drowning* by Kwame
Owusu at the Bush.

Africa Blagrove
Africa Blagrove is an Assistant Stage Manager from Northwest/
West London. She started her stage management journey towards
her last year of college when she applied for a stage
management work placement with *Get Up! Stand Up! The Bob Marley
musical*.

Early last year, Africa joined the RADA Youth company on the
technical theatre pathway where she gained skills in all
technical aspects and was the Stage Manager/Head of Props for
Alice in Wonderland which was put on at RADA with the Young
Company Acting pathway.

Her ASM credits include: *#Blackis…* (New Diorama Theatre) and
Get Up! Stand Up! The Bob Marley Musical (Lyric Theatre).

'The Yard Theatre is a mecca for some of the most interesting theatre in Britain.' *British Vogue*

The Yard reimagines theatre. Our programme crosses genres and breaks boundaries, because the artists we work with want to say something new, in new ways. We work with artists who reflect the diversity of East London, who tell new stories. They invite us into journeys of escape, euphoria, possibility and hope. Through this The Yard reimagines the world.

We've developed artists like Michaela Coel, Alexander Zeldin, Marikiscrycrycry and Dipo Baruwa-Etti, Yard Young Artists like Lamesha Ruddock and nightlife collectives like INFERNO and Pxssy Palace. They've all used their vision and energy to give us new stories and narratives for what the world could be.

Recent work includes: ★★★★★ *The Flea* written by James Fritz, directed by Jay Miller (2023), ★★★★★ *An unfinished man* written by Dipo Baruwa-Etti, directed by Taio Lawson (2022), *The Cherry Orchard*, reimagined by Vinay Patel, directed by James Macdonald (2022), ★★★★★ *The Crucible* written by Arthur Miller, directed by Jay Miller (2019), ★★★★★ *Dirty Crusty* written by Clare Barron, directed by Jay Miller (2019), ★★★★ *Armadillo* written by Sarah Kosar, directed by Sara Joyce (2020), ★★★★ *A New and Better You* by Joe Harbot, directed by Cheryl Gallacher (2018) and ★★★★★ *Buggy Baby* by Josh Azouz, directed by Ned Bennett (2018).

theyardtheatre.co.uk
@theyardtheatre

SAMUEL TAKES A BREAK…
IN MALE DUNGEON NO. 5
AFTER A LONG BUT GENERALLY
SUCCESSFUL DAY OF TOURS

Rhianna Ilube

Acknowledgements

Somebody once told me, 'build a community around your play' and this is what I have tried to do from the start.

I'd like to dedicate *Samuel* to my grandmothers, Gwen and Eileen, and my parents, Tom and Caron – I'm eternally thankful to you all, for the choices you made, and the worlds you showed me growing up.

Josephine, thank you for everything in those years and now. Shilpa, Lewis, Charlotte and Meera, thank you for the non-stop support, documented through our years of voice-notes.

Jessi, thank you for your tireless work to get this play on.

To all my friends & family who have read, motivated and provided love, thank you. Especially: Eugene, Linda, Isabelle, Callum, Gayathiri, Daniel, Violet, Eliza, Zoe, Lexine, Nina, Louna, Melissa, Selin, Diane, Selma, Roland, Pri, Aarti, Maria, Matthew, Alex, Anna and everyone else who has been there through it.

To the many people across the industry who have read, offered feedback, introduced me to someone, or advised me along some way, I truly appreciate it. Thank you to the Royal Court team and the support of the Intro Group – especially Miriam, Ellie, Jane, Hamish and Nkechinyere. To Marie at the Omnibus Theatre & my co-directors Josie and Tatenda for helping me develop the play there. To my Goldsmiths MA crew and teachers. To my friends at Coney. To the Sky Table Read team.

And of course, thank you to The Yard for giving *Samuel* the perfect home. Thank you Jay for taking on the play and the guidance throughout. To the incredible creative team for giving it everything to make this play the best it could be. To Anthony and Taiwo for your incredible minds and dedication, which has truly helped shape this play for the better. To Aïsha, Africa, Kia,

Johanna and everyone on the production team for your deep care throughout.

I am grateful to the many actors who have developed this play in workshops over the years, sharing your honest thoughts and willingness to experiment with the characters. To Fode, Tori, Stefan and Bola – I couldn't have dreamt for a better cast for *Samuel*'s first production, thank you for the love, care and insights you have given to this.

I've been to the castle many times. Been on many a walking tour. To all the people I've met over the years who are trying to find a way to remember and preserve these histories, I am thankful to you.

R.I.

'You've got to enjoy yourself. The evening's the best part of the day. You've done your day's work. Now you can put your feet up and enjoy it.'

Kazuo Ishiguro, The Remains of the Day

'You know they hate us, or haven't you figured that out yet?'

Saidiya Hartman, Lose Your Mother

'Think about laughter and what happens to your body – it's almost the same thing that happens to you when you throw up.'

Suzan-Lori Parks, Elements of Style

Characters

SAMUEL, *senior tour guide, Ghanaian. Male, mid-late twenties*
ORANGE, *ticket-booth assistant / aspiring tour guide, Ghanaian. Female, early twenties*
TREV, *tourist, Black British. Male*
LETTY, *tourist, mixed-race British. Female*

And a range of other TOURISTS, *many African-American, some West African and Black British. There should be only four actors.*

Some Notes on the Text

The description of the castle is more for the imagination, and does not need to be taken literally for set design.

'hahahaha's', 'hehe's, **bold text**, <u>underlined text</u>, etc., are also more indicative of tone, than literal.

/ and – generally mean overlapping or interrupted text.

A (*Rest.*) is more of a mood, and a *Beat.* is suggestive of rhythm.

This text went to press before the end of rehearsals and so may differ slightly from the play as performed.

ACT ONE. DAYTIME

An Ordinary Day of Tours Delivered by Samuel

Lights on. Take your seats.

As time goes on, we start to hear the sounds of chit-chat, footsteps, hawkers, cries…just, you know, the regular comings and goings of a slave castle in the summertime.

Gradually, we see the shape of a man standing emerge on stage.

This is SAMUEL.

SAMUEL *is dressed quite smartly, perhaps wearing a dark suit jacket, jeans and a watch. He holds his script at all times.*

SAMUEL *stands before us in his 'tour mode'. This means that he has taken on the weight of his task as a Storyteller and Preserver of History.*

He stares out. Tries to smile at us.

Does the smile work? No. He tries again.

Smiles.

Again?

Nope. Not today. Anyway. Oh well.

It's just another day at work.

SAMUEL *is standing in the courtyard of Cape Coast Castle, the former slave castle. This is an old castle overlooking the sea. It is faded white, dirty, cracked. But seen from a distance, the castle could be considered beautiful.*

There are three levels to this castle:

Underground *is where the dungeons are. This is where* SAMUEL *spends most of his time, as his work demands. The male dungeon is made up of five chambers. No light, no windows. Five chambers, one thousand men at any one time. Until a ship came. Etc.*

There is also a dungeon for women and children. Two chambers, four hundred women and children at any one time. Ventilation slots. Thanks.

There are other cells, for punishment.

The chambers are connected by underground tunnels. SAMUEL *spends his days navigating these tunnels when leading his tours.*

On ground level *is a courtyard. The courtyard overlooks the sea. We should hear the sea, it should be strongly present. It is almost as if the sea is watching, reacting to and even conducting the many events that take place here.*

Upstairs *is the governor's residence, and a church. The church is above the Male Dungeon No. 1. Yes, I'm not making this up. Upstairs is airy, light. Lots of windows. Views of the sea, of the beach.*

Most of SAMUEL*'s world is underground. Most of* ORANGE*'s world is on ground level. Nobody stays upstairs for long.*

Now that's sorted, back to SAMUEL. *He is ready to get on with… with…*

The Tour

Whenever you're ready, SAMUEL. *We'll start at the courtyard.*

SAMUEL   Hello you are welcome
                 to the first tour of my day. I'm
                 looking forward to
                 getting to know you
                 all
                 over the next hour
                 or so.

                 (*Rest.*)

                 My name is Samuel.

                 How does it feel?

To be here today.

Anybody? Anybody?

(Rest.)

Please… if you have any questions,
you know who to ask.

(Rest.) Tries to smile.

I would love to get to know
some of the people and places
you have all been travelling from.

Please, may I ask some people in here
to call out your names

and where you have travelled here from.

SAMUEL *engages in some light audience
interaction – collecting some names and
countries / locations of the people in the room.*

Ah!

It is so exciting to have such a diverse
range of people in front of my eyes.

It is why I do this job.

It is why I love this job.

(Rest.) An endearing smile.

You will all have travelled far and wide
to visit this humble house. The building
you stand before housed many… slaves
before they were sent on their way.

But please o, we don't like that word
'slave' here… thank you.

So join me in this action.
Throw the word – away.

*Gestures throwing the word away, without
much enthusiasm.*

Away!

Away!

Very good.

Yes, we have received feedback from several guests
that it is not a word that people like.

Mmm.

Now, each one of us will be here for
a different particular reason.
I am here because
I am passionate about history.

(*Rest.*)

Some of you will be the descendants
of the men and the women who
passed through these walls in shackles.

Mm-hm.

(*Rest.*)

Some of you may be the descendants
of those who sold them.

Mm-hm.

(*Rest.*)

Some of you will have no connection
at all. For you, this is just another day
at a general tourist site.
That is also good. But as for today,
we are on this tour,
and we are a family.
And we are one human family, glad to be reunited.
We will be learning and growing together.
Then you will go. Thank you.
Now please, if you will. We must enter the
first dungeon. For men.

Exit tour mode.

SAMUEL *stands still, looking out, rocking
slightly, trying to see something in the
distance. He is…fidgety.*

And he's back.

Next Tour

SAMUEL   Hello you are welcome
                to the second tour of my day. I'm
                looking forward to
                getting to know you
                all of you
                over the next hour
                or so.

                (*Rest.*)

                My name is Samuel.

                How do you feel?

                To be here today.

                Anybody? Anybody?

                (*Rest.*)

                Please… if you have any questions,
                you know who to ask.

                (*Rest.*)

                I would love to know
                where some of you have
                been travelling from.

                Please, call out your names and say where
                you are from…

                SAMUEL *engages in some light audience
                interaction – collecting some names and
                countries / locations of the people in the
                room.*

                His eyes are slightly glazed over.

                Ah!

                It is so nice to see many many different
                people here.

                It is why I do this job.

                It is why I love this job.

                (*Rest.*) *Time moves on.*

So join me in this action, please.

Throw the word – away.

Away!

Away!

Very good.

Exit tour mode.

And he's back.

Next Tour

SAMUEL   Hello you are welcome
to my
third tour of the day.
I am very happy very looking
forward to – to getting to know
you over the next hour.

(*Rest.*)

How does it feel?

(*Rest.*)

You have all travelled miles
to visit this honourable
improbable castle. The building
you stand
before imprisoned many many slaves

Considers throwing the word 'slave'
away. Dismisses it – let's mix things up,
he thinks.

before they were sent off on their way.

(*Rest.*)

Very good.

Each one of us will be here for a
special, unique reason.
Some of us will be the descendants
of the slaves who passed
through in shackles,
chains, blood dripping from their
feet and hands.

To you, we say: welcome!

Some of us may be the descendants of those
who sold them.

To you, we say: why did you do that ? Ha.

(*Rest.*)

You are my family.

If you follow me, to the first dungeon please.
For men.

He is cut off by a young American tourist.

TONI   Do you wish... secretly, that you could've
            been one of them? Or – I mean – your
            ancestors? Because then you would be
            American.

SAMUEL   Or Jamaican. Or British.

TONI   Exactly!

SAMUEL   No I do not wish that.

Next Tour

SAMUEL   Welcome home.

How do you feel?

To be here today?

Anybody?

Silence.

My name is Samuel, and I will be your tour guide for today. In fact, you are all lucky. Do you know why? It is also my birthday. This is a birthday tour.

Sings. Encourages the room to sing for him.

Happy birthday to me…

Next Tour

SAMUEL   Oh, yes, that's nice to hear that you are thinking of moving to Ghana.

MARGARET   I am. I just – I can't do it any more. America, no. Nuh-uh. I don't want to be there. This was where I was taken from. So I should be with you. I'm at home here. Year of Return baby. I'm back. With you. We are siblings, reunited, at last.

SAMUEL   Yes please. Thank you for coming back. It is an honour to greet you here.

Beat.

My sister.

She gets emotional.

MARGARET   Sorry Samuel. Sorry – could I. Could I get your WhatsApp?

SAMUEL   Um, pardon me?

MARGARET   Your WhatsApp, Samuel. Just – just put it in
                here. I'm gonna need community when I put
                down roots here.

SAMUEL   Oh okay. Yes.

                Ehm,

                I don't usually give out my personal details

MARGARET   Oh, Samuel – don't worry about it – I'm not
                gonna spam you or anything – I just need
                a friendly contact in the vicinity. You know
                what I mean?

SAMUEL   Oh yes, yes of course.

                Anything for a new member of this country.

                Here you go –

                He gives his number.

Next Tour

*American tour group. Matching T-shirts: 'Africa for the
Africans'.*

SAMUEL   At the end I will take you through the Door of
                No Return

                but this time, I assure you

                Beat.

                you will return.

                Beat.

                haha. ha.

KEITH   Excuse me Samuel.

SAMUEL   Yes sir.

KEITH   Excuse me Samuel, but I am not sure that that is an appropriate joke to make.

SAMUEL   I am sorry sir. It is not a joke sir.

KEITH   Sorry Samuel. I'm sorry. I am struck by the gravity of this place. I am simply shocked, Samuel

by the things you have told me today.

But I believe I am speaking on behalf of my brothers and sisters here when I say I am also shocked

at the way you choose to

speak

to us, like this, in this place.

SAMUEL   Sir /

KEITH   We are here to connect with you, Sam.

To rebuild those bridges, you know. I want us all to be respectful of why we are here. Including yourself. So

If you don't mind Samuel, I'd like to take moment to just

bring this tour back together

bring us all back together now

and ground us in this place.

Beat.

do you mind if I take a moment to do that Samuel?

SAMUEL *does mind, but says nothing.*

Thank you.

Lunch Break with Orange, the Ticket-Booth Assistant

ORANGE *and* SAMUEL *usually have their lunch together.* ORANGE *being the charismatic and enigmatic ticket-booth assistant, on a national service placement.*

They are sitting in the staff lunch area. It's round the back, guests would never usually see this place.

They eat for a while in a comfortable silence. Then, just like clockwork:

SAMUEL   So how is it going. In the ticketing booth?

              ORANGE *ignores him. She's eating. He always asks her this question and today she's thinking like, 'Oh come on, Samuel, say something interesting.'*

              'It's good Samuel, thanks. How is your day going?'

              ORANGE *looks up.*

              This is not typical of SAMUEL *– the sarcasm, I mean.*

ORANGE   Haha.

              Eh. I like this Samuel. Fun Samuel. You think you are funny eh.

SAMUEL   It is because it is my birthday.

              Beat.

ORANGE   Is it true? You are lying.

SAMUEL   It is.

ORANGE   Nooooo. Ah! You are getting old. And you didn't tell me! The way I love birthdays too.

SAMUEL   Yes.

ORANGE   So you were born –

SAMUEL   Yes.

ORANGE   You were born in –

SAMUEL   It is my Year-of-Return birthday.

ORANGE	But if it is actually your birthday
	your real birthday
	then we need to do something, or?
SAMUEL	I have plans.
ORANGE	Ah you are rude o. Which plans at all do you have.
SAMUEL	They don't involve anybody within the castle staff.
	I don't mix business with pleasure.
ORANGE	That's weird to say.
SAMUEL	Okay.
	And you, how old are you again?
ORANGE	Twenty-one.
SAMUEL	Ahh.
	Yes. That makes sense.
ORANGE	Me and Arabella are thinking of going out on Saturday
SAMUEL	Oh nice… that's cool. Cool.
ORANGE	Do you want to come?
SAMUEL	No no. I've got a lot of reading to do.
ORANGE	What are you reading?
SAMUEL	I am reading *The Best of Phillis Wheatley*…
ORANGE	Eh why are you reading slavery stuff on a Saturday.
SAMUEL	Who told you it is slavery 'stuff'.
	Well it is slavery stuff.
	But it is important Orange.
	It is what distinguishes me from Julie.
	It is why Doris appointed me to edit this –

ORANGE	Julie is coming on Saturday.
SAMUEL	Exactly.
ORANGE	Do you ever leave the castle Samuel?
SAMUEL	Yes.
ORANGE	Like do you ever really leave the castle Samuel?
SAMUEL	Yes.
ORANGE	Because I never see you leave.
SAMUEL	I leave. Every day. Don't we walk out together.
ORANGE	Yeah but

Why do I get the sense that you don't actually leave.

Like. Does that make sense.

Beat.

When I'm your age I'll be out of here.

'Good morning Ghana. The sun is shining and you are locked in with me, your favourite and most loved host.'

You will be watching me on TV every day, from here. You will be thinking: 'I used to work with her. Wow.'

SAMUEL	I will be too busy to watch you.
ORANGE	Ooookay.

I find out today.

SAMUEL	Eh?
ORANGE	The application. You have forgotten! You don't care about me! I hear back today.
SAMUEL	Ohhhh. Yes.

Beat.

How are you feeling about it.

ORANGE	Very good. No stress.
	I am sure it will be a yes. I cannot wait to be out of here! My first steps to TV presenting. Ah. I was born for it.
	And that will just be the start. In ten years or so,
	I'll be living in
	New York.
	As a public speaker. Or something.
	You can visit me.
	Maybe.
	I'll take you to Times Square. And Brooklyn.
SAMUEL	You know what.
ORANGE	What
SAMUEL	Do you know what.
ORANGE	Whattttttttt.
SAMUEL	I think you'll be here.
ORANGE	Ah!!
SAMUEL	For many many more years.
ORANGE	??
SAMUEL	Oh yes. That is the general trajectory.

ORANGE *looks downcast for a moment.* SAMUEL *doesn't take the hint.*

Don't hope too much for success. Your application video was satisfactory but there will have been many other applicants. You have a good job here. It is stable. It is important. You meet many people. You have the possibility to grow in the role. Yes. Far more important than presenting. Be content with what you have... If you do not get the news you were hoping for, you should not worry too much.

Maybe one day, you will be a tour guide. Like me.

ORANGE   I will get it. No problem. But even when I get it, the internship will not start for a few months. So…

Beat.

Samuel I had a question

SAMUEL   Mm.

ORANGE *falters.*

ORANGE   Do you – do you…

No. Not yet. Now isn't the time. Divert.

ever want to hurt the tourists?

SAMUEL   Huh?

ORANGE   Or like. Slap them or something.

SAMUEL   No.

ORANGE   Not all o. Just some. One or two. Seriously. You're a robot. Seriously.

Because come on. Some of them can be soooo –

SAMUEL   You must practise empathy Orange. Put yourself in their shoes.

ORANGE   …

SAMUEL   Yes

this is a day that each tourist will never forget

they will never forget you Orange. Well. They might forget you but they will never forget me. As their tour guide.

Beat.

Do not speak like that of the tourists. It was quiet before you came, before the Year of Return.

Sometimes we would sit here all day, and nobody would even come. I would do two, three tours a day. And I used to feel tired then. Ah!

So even though, yes. Yes… they do – they are – annoying – at times.

I just try and maintain my composure. I let my steam off in other ways.

ORANGE   How do you let your steam off Samuel?

And it can't just be your biscuit breaks.

SAMUEL   In fact my biscuit breaks are

are – are

are useful. For letting go.

When I am eating those biscuits I am happy.

ORANGE   You need to enjoy yourself.

You really need to just. Yes. Let go. Take it easy.

SAMUEL   Orange. I let go. I relax. I chill.

ORANGE   We need to celebrate Samuel, have some fun.

That they made it here. That any of them made it here at all.

SAMUEL   …

ORANGE   Aaaaand that it is your birthday. Aaaand that it is the day I find out

that I am leaving

this place!

Beat.

You can't just be sad all of the time. Smile Samuel!

SAMUEL   I'm not /

ORANGE   Were you like this as a small boy?

SAMUEL   Like how?

Beat.

You – don't worry. One day you will
become a serious one too

ORANGE: *face of disbelief.*

you will

you will only understand once you qualify

and become an actual

tour guide.

ORANGE: *yesyesyes heard this before.*

SAMUEL *continues, as he was, as if in
a sort of… reverie.*

I was actually once described, Orange, as

Beat.

'fun loving'.

Beat. Then:

ORANGE   Who described you as fun loving????
ahhahahah

hahzhahahhahadsfh

ahhahahashdfhahahhahaha

SAMUEL   My mother please

we would come up here

'let's go to the castle'

we would come here and watch the tourists
come in and out and she'd go up and talk to
them

or she would force me to

said I'd become a better person

more intelligent

open, cultured

if I spoke to the

British

Dutch

Spanish

French

American

African-American

Mm-hm. We loved them.

People of the

other

African

nations

stories of our family members taken

taken in the castle, lost in the castle

said we might hear them if we stayed close,

we might honour them if we stayed close.

He breaks.

And the tourists, oh the tourists! We used to
sell them toys, we used to make them pay /

ORANGE   Alright alright Sam but why do all your
stories come

back to the castle?

I swear one day we need to meet up outside of
this place

it isn't good for our blossoming friendship

Beat.

Stand up Samuel.

SAMUEL   No. I am comfortable.

ORANGE	Stand up. Come on.
SAMUEL	I am fine Orange. I am fine.

ORANGE imparts her secret powers of persuasion.

Up he gets.

ORANGE	Let goooooooo.

Samuel,

okay Samuel.

We've got to listen to Orange.

For once.

SAMUEL	Am letting go.
ORANGE	Ooooookay.

Ooooooookayyyyyyyyy.

Slaveryyyyyy

is not the

be-alllll

and end-alllll

of life.

Life is about enjoyment.

Repeat that after me, Samuel.

Beat.

SAMUEL	Life is about enjoyment.

For a moment, SAMUEL lets go. Blink and you'll miss it.

Next Tour

Older British-Jamaican woman and SAMUEL. *They are looking at a map detailing where the enslaved people were mostly sent to from the castle.*

JERRI   Now Samuel,
                         My family, that's where we're from – do you
                         remember me talking
                         about that – that's
                         where we're
                         from…
                         so they were most likely
                         most likely taken from
                         here Samuel? Is that right.

SAMUEL   Yes – we have records that show that. This
                         map here –

JERRI   Oh. My my. Baby.
                         Mummy would've liked to have seen this,
                         wouldn't she.

                         It was here then.
                         It was here. Where they were.

                         Could I have a moment, Samuel?

SAMUEL   Of course. I will stand here.

                         She starts to speak to them. Her ancestors.

JERRI   Hello
                         Hello
                         Can you hear me?
                         I'm Jerri
                         Been waiting my whole life to be here
                         to talk to you
                         what to say?
                         thank you
                         thank you for getting through it
                         for your
                         your children
                         for your life
                         I'm sorry
                         I'm here

I'm okay
Things are okay
We have a big family now
There's lots of us, the kids are doing well
Kay is having a baby girl next month
Oh. And Stevie passed just a few weeks ago…
But. You know this already don't you.
It's alright, it's alright, he had a long long life.
England, we went there.
Yes. I'm doing okay now

SAMUEL *watches quietly.*

Next Tour

We are in the gift shop. There's lots of gifts in here.

SAMUEL	Welcome to the gift shop
	Here you may buy many commodities
	My personal favourite is this book here, written by my great mentor and old teacher, Dr Kwame Nelson, a popular historian of this castle and the man who truly gave me my first break here when I was simply a young man. I am so grateful. God bless him.
	In fact I have memorised the entire introduction of his biography…
	He is drowned out.
SHELLY	Oh these fans are great
SAMUEL	Oh, madam, I think there are much better things to look at /
MARK	How many do you want love? Five? Ten?
SHELLY	Get them all –
MARK	Alright Sam ten fans, how much is that. Can we get a deal, ten for nine?

SAMUEL *sadly places down Dr Kwame's
book. Nobody purchases this book, ever.
Which is a shame, because it is actually quite
a good book.*

He counts out ten fans, a little ruefully.

Orange at the Ticket Booth

Let's turn our attention once again to ORANGE, *this time
alone. She is sat in the ticket booth tucked in the entrance of
the castle.*

ORANGE*'s role is to check in new guests and hand them
a 'Year of Return' pamphlet. She longs for* SAMUEL*'s job.
This job is boring.*

*The ticket box has been decorated. 'Happy Year of Return'
paraphernalia.*

ORANGE *is practising what she wants to tell* SAMUEL.

ORANGE   Hey Samuel

                Samuellllll… Sammie…. Sammmm…
                Samooooo… Samito… eh big Samuel –

                okay Orange. you need to relax. Samuel – he
                does not respond to…

                Snaps fingers.

                emotion.

                'I was thinking it would be good if I could get
                some experience for my presenting…'

                no.

                'I was meaning to ask you.'

                Noo. Oh Orange, you too. Be serious.

Eh. Samuel.

…

give me your tours.

Samuel

nobody likes your tours.

no. haha.

Samuel…

you need me to save this /

ORANGE *sees the audience* (*aka tourists*).

oh. sorry o, I didn't see you all

hellooooo everyone. my name is Orange

Happy Year of Return

we are grateful you're here, sister.

the cost is twenty cedis

Ten dollars

Fifteen pounds

Thirty if you want to use a camera

Year-of-Return price.

please wait there

your tour guide Julie will be here shortly

welcome to the castle

my name is Orange

Happy Year of Return

we are grateful that you are here.

you must pay twenty

Thirty if you want to use a camera

please wait there

Kwesi your tour guide will be here shortly

oh madam! I like your top, you are looking good o

for you I will lower the price

Sees the accompanying man. Urgh.

oh, I am sorry. are you with this man?

Beat.

mm-hm.

then you must both pay thirty each.

thank you

Next Tour

TOURIST LEADER   Ghana called and said come home, so we did.

TOURIST   Yes we did!

Can we get an Amen?

ALL   Amen!

TOURIST LEADER   God bless us all here today, and thank you to our tour guide, Mr Samuel. Please. As the leader of the Soul Festival delegation, I wanna say a few words. We have brought together some of the finest members of the African diaspora to see Ghana, reconnect with our roots here, and look for places to invest in. Our ancestors were taken. We can't avoid that fact. But we are back, with money!

They cheer.

And I know it is a dark topic to bring up but we do need to talk about the C-word

that is

complicity

Com-pli-city

of the Ghanaian people themselves

TOURIST LEADER *looks pointedly at* SAMUEL.

SAMUEL   Oh

TOURIST   It was not you Samuel, no, I'm not coming for you now, but I am just saying us descendants, we do need to rebuild some bridges of harm between those who stayed.

SAMUEL   Oh, yes sir, I am very committed to rebuilding the bridges of harm

TOURIST   Okay Samuel. Okay.

              Let us pray, y'all.

Samuel Imagines a Future for Himself Outside of the Castle

We see SAMUEL. *Corner of the courtyard. A quiet moment in the shade.*

And I think this scene exists here because SAMUEL *wants to think outside of the castle, breathe outside of the castle and so here he is, and he wants to imagine – just for a day – that he doesn't have to stay here.*

He looks over to the sea – the same sea – and it is like he hears something we can't hear, he starts to say something back, we listen but we can't –

Afternoon Break: Orange and Samuel, Again

ORANGE *is suddenly by his side.*

ORANGE	If you could do one thing in the castle, what would it be?
SAMUEL	What do you mean?
ORANGE	Like I would
	I think I would
	I would
	She whispers something scandalous to SAMUEL
SAMUEL	Ah! You are bad o.
ORANGE	Yeah.
SAMUEL	Oh no no no.
ORANGE	Sorry.
	Beat.
	I don't want to offend your sensibilities.
SAMUEL	It's okay.
	Beat.
	So where would you do it?
ORANGE	Eh?
SAMUEL	Never mind. Sorry. Was just a
	logistical –
	don't worry.
	Beat.
	Which tourist would you –
	today –
	which one?

ORANGE	There's a new one
SAMUEL	Oh yeah
ORANGE	Actually no
SAMUEL	Mm.
ORANGE	I changed my mind. The eleven forty-five a.m.
SAMUEL	Oh.
ORANGE	Yeah.
SAMUEL	I didn't see.
ORANGE	You were too busy looking at your notes.
SAMUEL	I was not looking at my notes!
ORANGE	Sometimes I look at you and you are always looking at your notes
SAMUEL	You are lying.

He looks up at the audience, for backup? Audience most likely does nothing.

ORANGE	Your head is always like
	' '

ORANGE demonstrates SAMUEL's head during tours.

when you're doing your tours

SAMUEL	No no no you're lying.

My head is held up high.

ORANGE is internally like lol.

I don't

I don't like to –

objectify

ORANGE	Eyyy brofo! Big words.
SAMUEL	The tourists
ORANGE	No.
	No.
	Of course.
	Me too
SAMUEL	You shouldn't –
	You shouldn't do that.
	You should focus.
ORANGE	There is one thing that would help me focus more…

She is cut off.

Next Tour

The condemned chamber. No room to move. (Note: MAN is Nigerian.)

SAMUEL	We have reached it.
	The dungeon for the twelve.
	This is the condemned chamber.
	some captives here made an attempt fighting
	for their freedom.
	some captives made an attempt here
	of escaping,
	yes. those who made the attempts were caught
	to be condemned in here.

the British wished to make an example of the troublesome ones.

there is evidence that the captives in the condemned chamber

condemned chamber condemned chamber the condemned –

went through a certain hell.

A long pause.

MAN   (*Aside.*) Is this it?

SAMUEL   Yes.

I'm going to lock you in this room for twelve minutes.
So you can experience the true

experience

This is a new addition to the script.

Then I'll set you free. Haha.

SAMUEL *switches off the lights.*

We start to hear hints of the true

'experience'

then:

MAN   Eh Samuel! Eh –

Let us out o! I am not a slave

I am not a slave I am a free man o

ahahhahahahah

I am a free man

hahahahhahaha

ow

what –

Knocking sounds:

'Please, please, let us out.'

…

SAMUEL *lets them out.*

Everyone is pissed. They might mutter, etc.

SAMUEL   Is everything alright?

MAN   Yes yes, ah, of course, twelve minutes is not enough, please.

Final Tour

KERRY, *a vlogger from the UK, is on the tour with* SAMUEL. *She is live-streaming the below, outside the Door of No Return.*

KERRY   Andddddddddd

welcome everyone – it is great to have you all here today.

I'm Kerry – most of you know who I am – and thank you to everyone who has been following my trip so far.

As with every live, I want to start with a moment to breathe.

let's breathe, in

and out

in and out

She gets SAMUEL *in the frame.*

Samuel – come on, with me now, in and out

that's great.

Yes, everyone – wow, looks like we've got
a good almost five thousand people watching
right now, that's brilliant, tell your friends to
get involved…

yes – I am with Samuel, who has been
giving me a brilliant tour of the truly
disturbing Cape Coast Castle. And as
promised, I will be live-streaming my walk
through the Door of No Return, where we
are stood now.

SAMUEL   Yes. Yes we are – I can tell your viewers a bit
about the door /

KERRY   Yes yes, but let's not rush into things, no, let's
let them hear a bit about YOU.

SAMUEL   Oh okay.

Between the questions below, SAMUEL *may
try to answer – but to no avail.*

KERRY   How long has it been? Working here, where
did you grow up, what's your hobbies outside
of the castle, do you have a wellness practice
– it must be very important for you working
here…

SAMUEL   Oh well I…

KERRY   and you know, what does the Year of Return
really mean to you.

I mean, REALLY mean. Because it feels like
more than just a tourism initiative, a money
thing; no – it REALLY feels like this was the
year. Do you see what I mean, Samuel. That
this. was. the year.

SAMUEL   yes – well, okay, um, I will start with

question number one, yes, for your viewers –
hello everybody –

Mmmm

Looks almost heartbroken for a moment.

My name is Samuel. I have been working at this castle for three years. Talking about the history of the coast and the slavery activity that took place here.

Fidgets. His voice starts to speed up. He is more animated than we have seen him previously, and acts almost urgently.

I – I aspire to one day manage this castle. And receive funds from the people watching this video, to help improve upkeep.

I intend to improve the tunnel right here. Come here, please, I will show you, for your viewers.

He brings KERRY *to the blocked-up tunnel.*

I would say that my aspiration is to remove these bricks. So we can experience the reality of the actual walk they took out to the sea. The British filled up the tunnels with bricks when they left...

KERRY   Why would they do that?

SAMUEL   Good question! We think to prevent the castle being taken over. Yes. We cannot do their final walk. This is a shame. This is a grand shame. Yes. I want this tour to be an accurate experience of what the sla– enslaved went through.

Beat.

I want to create a historically accurate tour.

KERRY   Thankkkk you, that's wonderful. Oh we have some questions coming through

people are interested in your recommendations Samuel – oh, Elia from

Norwich is asking for – for your skin-care
regime, yes, we all need to know a bit of that.

SAMUEL   Oh, um

I – I have much more to say on the door – and
your past questions, the Year of Return,
firstly –

KERRY   Oh! Another question in! Laurie and Frank
will be coming over from Germany in
October – they are asking for
recommendations of places to sleep when in
Cape Coast, could you –

SAMUEL   yes yes but, okay, but if I am taking the
questions one at a time…

um, okay, hello everybody

KERRY   Oh another question, keep them coming!

*She gets absorbed in the feed… whilst she
is reeling off questions,* SAMUEL *will be
slowly saying the below – overlapping to
an extent:*

Okay Dominique wants book
recommendations Samuel, for her
homecoming book club… And forget the
skin-care tips, and also, you know, it would
be good if you know tailors in the area, and
my viewers would love to know some places
for a good massage or R&R if you know what
I mean, oh and back to the history… thanks
for putting us on course, Louisa! – can you
tell us about this door, for our viewers before
I do the walk?

SAMUEL   I grew up here.

By the castle. Yes.

With my mother.

And I am waiting.

*He is falling into a daydream or his own
world, for a moment.*

I am waiting for my mother.

KERRY   Oh!

Is she okay?

SAMUEL   Yes! Yes yes. I don't know why I – forget
what I am saying.

She will be coming soon, I am certain.

The door the door...

SAMUEL *suddenly snaps out of it, realises
he has said too much.*

You may walk through the Door of Return now.

Your viewers may have heard of this very
famous door

where one person would walk through at
a time.

now brothers and sisters in the diaspora can
come back

the door has been replaced.

yes.

it is now the Door of Return

you can now

return.

As a tour guide, it is my duty to ensure that
every tourist in my care passes through, and
returns back – unlike their ancestors. Their
ancestors have been waiting for this moment
for perhaps four hundred years.

That is a responsibility I take very seriously.

KERRY	You're talking very fast aren't you, just breathe, yes? I can see you're very tense, let me

She starts to massage him, it feels weird.

That's it. You'll be okay, it must be so much

doing this job

SAMUEL	Oh no I am very happy here, it is an honour to preserve...
KERRY	I think it's about time!
SAMUEL	Oh yes?
KERRY	Yes! For my walk, Samuel, will you hold this?

He holds the camera... and sees all the comments flooding in of people watching himself and KERRY.

Hold it like that... that's great, yes

Keep breathing, film and keep breathing, in and out, in and out.

SAMUEL *breathes. He may turn the camera to himself for a moment and say:*

SAMUEL	Ah – Goodbye everyone. Goodbye. Happy Year of Return.
KERRY	I'm walking! I'm doing the walk – you got this Samuel? You got it – everyone – look...

But mostly, he is breathing. It gets more intense, we hear him breathing. In and out. Heart beating. Something isn't right today. As he watches her go through the door and disappear, slowly the words of tourists, past and present, the words of her viewers, the words of everyone start to flood until he can no longer see her, or anything, for a moment. SAMUEL's *lines are underlined.*

Hello

my name is   from   my first tour of the day

I can't hear him I can't hear him can't hear what's he saying

> Excuse me? Sorry? Man. Samuel? Could you speak
>   up please?

family reunited

Very emotional   Always wanted to visit here

> Ancestors

Sir. We can't hear you at the back. Please far and wide

just enough to keep them alive   how did they sleep

dropped down ceiling

> Don't you want us to feel something?

>> Can't hear you urinating at the back speak
>> louder

> please. No cash no cash on me sorry
>> Watch your heads follow me   Tell it

Samuel!

> It was not me.   see these white marks

I don't want to go in there. Can I have a break? Break? break?
Don't worry Samuel

> Do you have photos?   Sorry remains?   I love it
>   here.

Julie!   Meeting people like   Hi my name is and I'm from
Atlanta Boston

> North Carolina and we are a family.

Uh-huh tell it!   and we are one human family

London want to be here have always wanted to be here it took me
five hours to get here do you know where we can eat.

Silence. silence in here can you be quiet?   We'll see you soon
> Samuel

menstruating

how many   may humanity never perpetuate such injustice

strong   ship   take?

can I film you? you?   <u>tied to trees, or a wild</u> <u>animal will</u>
                            <u>feast on you</u>

It's Samuel. Please. I'm just trying to do my job <u>those who</u>
<u>denied</u> here, sir. I've already <u>sexual advances</u> done

            Now. Is this a personalised or a standardised tour?

Will you sit down on the floor.   <u>have the museum</u>

ancestors wanted me to he moves like a <u>if i decide to jump</u>
<u>overboard,</u>

<u>i'm going to drag you into the ocean</u>.   slave

what did he say?

                            they told me

<u>Samuel</u> we can't see

                    ceiling

Can we turn the lights on <u>different particular</u> <u>reasons.</u>
                                    tell us Samuel

Is he locking us? are we being locked? Oh my god raindrops

        Hi I'm from from this place   this place don't
                                            know where I'm

<u>those who came</u> <u>after a ship</u> <u>could lie down</u> can't breathe
                    <u>questions?</u>

from how long will we be in here i can't breathe   Samuel
stop stop moves like a now just

                        a

                fishing please open

                        village the door

I am a free man   You can't stop

eh

    stop stop stop louder please for those of us who can't

            Where can I get

            water?

            End of Act One.

ACT TWO. EVENING

Samuel Takes a Break in Male Dungeon No. 5 After a Long But Generally Successful Day of Tours

In this scene, we observe SAMUEL *alone. He is in his end-of-day break area, a quiet corner of Dungeon No. 5. No one bothers him here, usually.*

SAMUEL *snacks on some biscuits. His daily treat. He sips juice from a straw.*

He takes his time. He looks out at us.

Sips his juice.

He eats another biscuit.

This can take a while.

Mm.

Then he starts to reflect on the events of the day.

SAMUEL   'We are here to connect with you, Sam.

                  To rebuild those bridges, you know.

                  I want us all to be respectful of why
                  we are here. Including yourself. So

                  If you don't mind Samuel, I'd like to take
                  a moment to just

                  bring this tour back together

                          bring us all back together now

                                  and ground us in this place.'

                  Beat.

                  'do you mind if I take a moment to do that
                  Samuel?'

                  SAMUEL *enjoys remembering this moment.*

To connect! With you. Ah!

Amen.

And do you know what?

I don't want to connect with you. Eh! So you
can –

Beat.

no.

'I want to hug you Samuel.'

is that connection

a hug?

Do you want a hug sir. Is that what you
want?

I can do that for you.

Mmmm.

Very good sir. I will just lock you

in here.

Nicely in here.

Mmmmmmm.

hehehe.

Back to his snacks. That was fun, wasn't it?

His alarm clock goes off. Six p.m.

He switches it off.

*He stands up and considers his posture. We
see his usual 'tour mode' stand.*

*He alters it a bit. Like, maybe he should stand
a bit more relaxed.*

*He alters it a bit. Like, maybe he should stand
a bit more powerfully.*

He alters it a bit. Like, maybe his face should be more stern.

I'm here to connect with you all

every single one of you

grounded in this tour.

We are all grounded in this tour

'And who are you Samuel?

Because who are you? Really?'

Why, I'm Samuel.

Yes.

I am Samuel.

and you are welcome

to my tour.

ORANGE enters. She watches him for a bit. Maybe she's been here a while and we didn't notice.

ORANGE   Eh Samuel, what are you doing!

SAMUEL freezes. She goes to stand by him.

I was looking for you. I missed you in here the first time.

Silence.

Were you performing or something?

like –

eh, relaxed Samuel. Were you pretending to be a slave?

Silence.

SAMUEL   …no.

ORANGE   Because you know I think it might not be a bad idea. I had once considered telling Doris to bring in some actors.

SAMUEL	Would that be a good idea, Orange?
ORANGE	I could even do it.
SAMUEL	No, no.
	Beat.
ORANGE	Okay okay. Soooooo. How was the rest of the day?
SAMUEL	Same as usual.
ORANGE	Arabella is doing forty people right now. Why aren't you helping?
SAMUEL	I've closed. Ten tours today. I never do more than ten tours a day. It is bad luck. You know that. And I am busy now. Can you see. I am perfecting the new tour.
ORANGE	Oooh. You know the beautiful lady in your last tour, the vlogger –
SAMUEL	Please, stop watching my tours.
ORANGE	What am I supposed to do. Eh. Anyway. Guess what.
	Beat.
SAMUEL	What
ORANGE	…
	We have the place to ourselves this weekend.
SAMUEL	What
ORANGE	I knowwwwww. Doris just told me. She is travelling somewhere. From tonight
SAMUEL	Eh
ORANGE	Sooooooo. I want to make party for you /
SAMUEL	We are not having a party
ORANGE	You could sing your song

SAMUEL   I do not sing.

ORANGE   But I hear you sing. Oh, I know!! We could
            hang out in the governor's bedroom –

SAMUEL   (*Sharply.*) Do not go in there. It is dangerous.
            Why is Doris leaving? Where is she going?
            Who is going to manage the castle?

ORANGE   I think she is leaving management in the
            hands of you.

SAMUEL   Please… nobody has informed me of this
            abeg.

ORANGE   Mm. Doesn't matter. You are now the boss.
            I defer to your orders, sah!

            SAMUEL *considers his new position for
            the weekend. He is quietly pleased.*

            Make I start the arrangements for the party
            tonight.

SAMUEL   No. No parties. I am busy tonight. I am
            editing the tour. I have plans.

ORANGE   Mm. But what about the new guests.

SAMUEL   What of them?

ORANGE   A new booking came in. For tonight. Two
            new guests from Britain. Good looking. They
            have requested the homecoming night-time
            tour. And they have requested for the tour to
            be led specifically by you.

            *This news both intrigues and unsettles him, as
            if he's been waiting for this.*

SAMUEL   Eh. Why didn't you tell me all this time?

ORANGE   They seem nice. I want to invite them to your
            birthday

SAMUEL   Ah, how?

ORANGE	So you need to get out of here. Ooooh. And thirdly
	Thirdly thirdly. One thing.
	Takes in a deep breath. This is it, let's do this properly.
	I would like to – to – to
	…
	switch roles this weekend
SAMUEL	Eh?
ORANGE	You ticket booth, me tours.
	Beat.
	I am bored o
	I am so bored.
	And seeing as we are now free and you are castle management
SAMUEL	Who are these guests /
ORANGE	So I thought now might be a good time for me to refine my touring
SAMUEL	Orange /
ORANGE	You know it is not easy. Spending all day at the ticketing office. Would you switch with me?
	Definitely not. Don't give in, Samuel.
SAMUEL	No please. I like being out there thank you
ORANGE	I am being discriminated against eh. Get in the box, give me one tour. I'd even do tonight if they hadn't asked for you. I don't know why they asked for you /
SAMUEL	You need to do the training if you don't know
ORANGE	Eh. It is just a script Samuel.

SAMUEL   It is <u>more</u> than just a script

ORANGE   'Welcome home, everybody. Welcome home,
              my African-American brothers and sisters'

SAMUEL   We don't refer to them in the familial terms
              unless they initiate that language first.

              Not strictly true.

ORANGE   'Welcome to the first male dungeon, follow
              me, heads down

              I assure you, this time, you will return'

              SAMUEL *thinks: Damn. She is quite good.*

SAMUEL   I will train you up one day. You have
              potential. But I can't just give you the tours
              just like that. They must be handled carefully.

              Now tell me more about this guest booking.

ORANGE   I don't know eh. They said they read your
              reviews and /

              SAMUEL *looks stressed.*

              Yes. I am surprised too. I respect you Samuel,
              I really do, but your reviews are not – they
              have been getting –

SAMUEL   Don't say it.

ORANGE   Well. Some people have found you a bit…
              recently.

SAMUEL   I'm asking about the guests /

ORANGE   What was that word?…

              Dry.

              Some people have found you a bit dry.
              Wearisome.

SAMUEL   What. Yes. Yes. I am aware of the reviews…
              ah.

Tries to ignore the bait. Can't.

What do people want from me eh? Full of life?

ORANGE   Nooo noooo. Eesh.

Pause.

Not full of life eh. But I think... maybe. Well.

when I look at you, sometimes I feel a bit...
You know.

SAMUEL   No.

Beat.

I do not do this job to please people. For every
one person who sees me as dry, there is another
who appreciates my commitment... my
commitment to the history. I am trying to
express the weight and the history of this place.

They come in here all of them not listening
they are eating they are crying and they are
wearing their little bracelets they bought from
Kwaku outside little beach hotel but they
don't know. They don't know. They want to
know where to eat afterwards. I say, how can
you eat after. Even the descendants, I don't
know. They look at me, and I don't want to
look in their faces any more and the couple
that couple I don't want to see them. I'm
working. Can you see. I've finished my ten.

ORANGE   I know I know. And it is very heavy. Yes
I mean it.

Anyway.

Please. Don't worry. Today there was no
problem. I watched your tours.

You did a very good job. Look, these people
want your tour. I don't know why. You must
appeal to them. It was just a couple of
things... nothing.

If you are feeling tired I'll do the tour... just give me the script eh.

She goes to get the script, and SAMUEL *jumps.*

SAMUEL No! No. You can't touch it, only qualified tour guides can touch...

ORANGE Yes yes okay fine.

Beat.

I didn't get the job.

SAMUEL Oh.

I am sorry.

ORANGE Yes. They just called. They said my tape had potential but there were many better applicants. They said I still need practise on my public speaking.

SAMUEL I did say –

ORANGE Don't say anything.

I will apply again. It is probably a mistake. I need to practise. Please Samuel, that's even more reason why I need to do some touring. I need to learn how to command an audience.

SAMUEL I just don't know. You are not ready. Anyway. Maybe you will get it next time.

Beat.

I am glad you are not leaving me though.

Maybe he does something unexpectedly tender, like put an arm around her.

ORANGE *looks at* SAMUEL *with her sad face. It works.*

Okay okay. You can come with me as I tour. It will be good experience for you and your aspirations.

ORANGE   Yes! Oooook. Thank you Samuel. So I will
                stand next to you. Like this. No distraction.
                And I have really been thinking. About how
                to improve our ratings. I care about you
                Samuel, and I have some ideas.

SAMUEL   Okay.

ORANGE   Okay?

                You want to hear my ideas?

SAMUEL   (*Reluctantly.*) Yes. Sure.

ORANGE   Okay. Well. Look. I've been watching you,
                the way you stand, the general aura you are
                giving off to the tourists.

SAMUEL   Why are you not just happy in your ticket
                booth. It is a –

ORANGE   Good job yes yes yes… please! Listen to me.

                Why don't we try this. I'll suggest some
                things to you. On the go. If I think you are not
                doing a good job. If I don't ever get the TV
                job maybe I will really focus on taking
                your job one day! As you say, being a tour
                guide… it is important work. I am so happy!

SAMUEL   I like to tour by myself.

ORANGE   I know I know. Thank you. Yes. You are the
                best. Happy birthday.

SAMUEL   I am coming. Tell them I am coming.

                SAMUEL *ruffles his papers – he is
                looking for the night-time tour script.*

                ORANGE *leaves.* SAMUEL *sighs a deep
                breath and sits back down to rest on the floor
                of Dungeon No. 5. He almost falls asleep.*

                *Maybe he sings a little, or hums in the
                darkness. Maybe he closes his eyes,*

murmuring to himself. Maybe he looks out at
us. He is in a dungeon, so there might be
a faint echo. We watch him.

Anyway. Enough of that.

Letty and Trev are Here for their Night-Time Tour

LETTY *and* TREV, *the tourists from the UK, are waiting for*
their tour to begin. She leans on him a bit. ORANGE *arrives.*

ORANGE   Hellooooo mister and missus. I have spoken
            to my colleague, my good friend, my mentor
            Samuel. He will be happy to tour you tonight.
            An extra tour. This is a little extra cost, but he
            will give you a discount. It is his birthday and
            he is in a good mood. It will be the tour of
            your lifetime.

LETTY   Oh exciting! Thank you!

ORANGE   Miss, you are welcome.

            Beat.

            I will also be accompanying the tour. I am
            training to become a tour guide.

            Beat.

            Please, before we start the tour, perhaps you
            can tell me a bit of what you are looking for
            today. Why are you here. What are you
            hoping for. And then we can tailor the tour to
            your specific circumstances.

LETTY   Okay, well. I'm Letty. This is my partner
            Trev –

TREV   Hello.

LETTY   What are we looking for, Trev?

TREV *shrugs a bit.*

TREV   You go ahead.

LETTY   Alright, well, okay.

I'm Letty

Don't travel much

Work in social care

My mum is Jamaican, Dad is British –
raised by him actually, Mum passed away
when I was –

anyway, yeah, I guess

I've always felt a certain emptiness in me?

This sense that something is gnawing at me,
like eating me, from inside, like

consuming me, like destroying me, a colossal
dread, breaking me down,

ruining me, from the inside, um

yeah

I don't even have my mum or her family to
ask you know

we were thinking of going to Jamaica on
holiday weren't we

to find my family, to find out where I'm from,
but then I thought

I don't even know where to start? With
myself?

I don't know who they are? Where they are?

So then, well, we just looked – heard about
this year here

and my friend came a few months ago and
since she's been back she

cannot stop talking about

Cape Coast Castle

She's always just like: 'Cape Coast Cape
Coast Cape Coast Cape Coast Cape Coast
Cape Coast Cape Coast'

and she was really moved by her tour guide,
she told me his name, showed

me a photo

here

Photo shown. It's Samuel.

that's why I thought – you know what, I'm
going to find him

this guy is my family, as much as anyone in
Jamaica is

you just never know, do you

so we're here, aren't we Trev

TREV   uh-huh

ORANGE   Oh okay. Yes, yes that is Samuel in the
photograph. Hm. Okay.

Mr Trev, you're very quiet. What are you
looking for

TREV   honestly –

Letty's heard this, she knows

I don't think that this was my idea of a dream
holiday

our last day in Ghana spent in a slave castle.

I don't think that's what I wanted

Do you know what, I – I… Letty, I think
I might actually sit this one out

Sort out the plan for later, start packing –
we've got a lot to think about –

LETTY	We spoke about this, it's just a restaurant –
TREV	Nah – I mean, you can go ahead, it's not as deep for me
LETTY	Sorry Orange one sec – Trev, I
	I do need you here
TREV	Alright. Alright, let's go.

Orange Goes Back to a Nervous Samuel

ORANGE *is bursting from excitement.*

ORANGE	Okay so they are ready.
SAMUEL	Okay.
	You have not told me what I am doing differently here.
ORANGE	Let me give you some information on them. Crucial intel.
	They appear to have relationship issues.
SAMUEL	Oh okay.
	What does that mean.
ORANGE	There is a tension. I just feel it.
SAMUEL	How is this relevant to the tour?
ORANGE	Okay it is not relevant but it is just contextual information. I thought it was interesting.
SAMUEL	Okay.
ORANGE	I don't know really, but I think she is unhappy in that relationship.
	SAMUEL *nods.*
	I felt in fact that perhaps she was looking at me.

SAMUEL   Stop it.

ORANGE   Look I am just saying.

            Another nod.

SAMUEL   Continue.

ORANGE   Okay so she is looking for her roots. Jamaican but not able to connect with that community. Raised by the whites. As for her man I am not sure. Unclear.

SAMUEL   What kind of information-gathering is this.

ORANGE   Sorry I was distracted.

SAMUEL   Okay so how am I supposed to improve my tour.

ORANGE   In general

            I think you need to be a little more personal. At the moment you are still so focused on your script and your little… improvisations, but you don't ask your tourists personal questions – like I have just done.

SAMUEL   Mm.

            That is because I am following Dr Kwame's training. Professionalism at all times. Not personal.

ORANGE   This is a new age. Year of Return. People are here for a very special occasion. If anything, Letty –

            Oh! I remember now. She is actually here because she thinks you are family.

            A bristle of hope.

SAMUEL   Family?

ORANGE   Metaphorically.

            Some person in London is talking a lot about you. Showing your photos.

So to her, to Letty, you are like a long-lost brother. Like she is trying to find you.

So you should act like one.

SAMUEL   Oh

Hm.

Okay.

Thank you Orange. That is good to know.

The Tour with Trev and Letty Begins

SAMUEL *and* ORANGE *meet* LETTY *and* TREV *at the courtyard.*

SAMUEL   Hello. My name is Samuel. This here is my colleague, Orange. I believe you have just met.

ORANGE   Madam.
                   Sir.
                   It is a pleasure.
                   You may call me 'O'. Miss O.

SAMUEL   Orange…

ORANGE   Oh sorry.

LETTY   Thank you Samuel, Orange – O. Honestly, I'm really sorry we are late –

                   but we are just so glad you fit us in today, and on your birthday! It's our last day in Ghana, isn't it Trev.

                   TREV *nods, seemingly tense.*

SAMUEL   Yes. Okay. You are welcome. Anything for my beloved brothers and sisters in the diaspora. I must admit, I do not normally do this extra tour but I thought – well – why not?

I am a year older. And some people say that it is good to spend your birthday evening in the company of other people. Family.

Yes.

LETTY   Yes! I don't think we have anything, do we, presents or whatnot, but – okay – oh god. That's a sign maybe. Surely, that's a sign. That, you know, I'm back here – it's your birthday, I dunno. This all feels very significant.

SAMUEL   Oh, maybe.

LETTY   Yeah! God, I feel like people are coming back from Ghana like, changed. Transformed. You know?

            She nudges TREV.

TREV   What? Oh, yeah – yeah.

            SAMUEL *starts ruffling his script, gets a little distracted.*

ORANGE   Ah! We are happy to have you! You will change here, there is no questions about it! We will change you! In fact, you will look in the mirror tomorrow and you won't even be able to recognise yourselves.

SAMUEL   Orange.

ORANGE   Oh sorry. Yes.

SAMUEL   Okay so, I will start the tour.

            Checks script.

            It is so exciting to have such a diverse range of people in front of my eyes.

            It is why I do this job.

            It is why I love this job.

(*To* LETTY.) Some of you will be the descendants of the men and the women who passed through these walls in shackles.

(*To* TREV.) Some of you may be the descendants of those who sold them.

TREV   Erm…

ORANGE   Oh sorry sir, he didn't mean to address that to you –

TREV   Yeah I just – sorry but – yeah, just – take it easy alright.

SAMUEL   Yes. Okay.

ORANGE   Greeeaaat. (*Whispers.*) Samuel – smile.

SAMUEL *smiles. Keeps checking his notes as he tours.*

SAMUEL   We are stood here in the courtyard, the location where many enslaved people were chained together before they were sent into their respective dungeons. As you can imagine, it was very hot /

LETTY   (*Whispers to* TREV.) Have you got my notebook?

TREV   Here

LETTY   Great

TREV   Alright

SAMUEL   Okay, um – we are on this tour,
and we are a family.
and we are one human family, glad to be reunited.
We will be learning and growing…

TREV   (*Under his breath.*) …we could've just gone to Jamaica

LETTY   I don't know my Jamaican family!!! and Samuel, Samuel? this is where it all started,

isn't it – like, what even is Jamaica, it's
here isn't it, my homeland, where I belong,
and and and we're here, you could have been
Jamaican, we could have all been Jamaican,
even you, Trev, if your family had… we
could've all had the last names

Smith

Jackson

Robins

Bell

Clarke

She gets out her notebook of questions from
TREV, *flicks through, and then:*

I'm here because this is where it's where it all
started and you know, it is just so emotional
to me, and you look familiar Samuel, you
know I'm not surprised it's your birthday
because when I looked at you, I thought: he
looks exactly like my cousin, could be twins
with my cousin, you look exactly like him
Samuel, and I guess that's what this place is
all about, I guess this is what this tour is all
about, finding people who look like you,
finding the people who looked like me,
finding the ancestors and asking them, what
was it like?

Would I have coped? Would you have coped?
I don't think we would've. We're not built
like that. Do you ever think about that? What
do you think?? I was reading a book I was
reading a book and the premise essentially
was that, it was a woman in her twenties, this
is a fictional book, it was a very good book,
but yes, it was all about – if she went back in
time, would she have survived. and this place
has got me thinking, Samuel. Would you have

survived? In here? Do you ever think about that? What do you think??

Beat.

SAMUEL   I do think about that.

From time to time.

Beat.

Yes, I think I would have survived.

An awkward pause.

Ah sorry. Would you like to go to the first male dungeon. Come with me.

In the Male Dungeon

SAMUEL   Welcome to the male dungeon, for five hundred men at a time.

If you look at the floor, you will see that you are standing on the faeces, the fossils, the blood, sweat, tears of the enslaved, of your ancestors, yes. Look closely, look at the floor

TREV   Sorry what time does this tour end by the way, cos we have a booking...

LETTY   Be patient Trev, come on!

TREV   I'm just keeping an eye on the time, we have...

SAMUEL   Er please, sorry, um

He looks desperately at ORANGE.

ORANGE   Samuel, tell our guests something you don't normally say on your tours. I promised them exclusive content!

SAMUEL   Okay. I can do that, yes. Well. Sometimes
          I like to spend time in here alone.

          Sometimes I feel like I can hear some of the
          people who were imprisoned here. For my
          research.

          Snaps out of it.

ORANGE   Thank you Samuel.

SAMUEL   No ventilation, please, look up, look at the
          window, no ventilation

          For a moment he is struggling to breathe.

          and they were standing the whole time – how
          did they sleep, sometimes I actually stand
          here and try to sleep, you know, because…

ORANGE   (*Whispers.*) Stand up straighter, more
          confidence

SAMUEL   Perhaps we can honour them? The men.
          A moment of silence.

ORANGE   Yes, I like it.

          A pause. Then:

SAMUEL   Thank you.

LETTY   this really just does hit home…

          You know what.

          I feel like this tour isn't enough – maybe we
          should all go and do something afterwards.
          We could extend the reservation… and just
          talk about everything.

          wouldn't that be nice Trev

TREV   Er, yeah – no, I wanted it to be just us…

LETTY   Tonight! After this tour, perhaps

          let's take them out, no?

	If it's your birthday after all, we can do something
	If you'd like that?
SAMUEL	Ah, thank you… but…
ORANGE	We would like that!
LETTY	Yes?!
ORANGE	Wouldn't we Samuel or?
SAMUEL	Please, erm – let us focus on the dungeon…
ORANGE	I've had an idea Samuel
SAMUEL	I think I no longer want your ideas.
ORANGE	I think you should let go of the script
SAMUEL	Ah –
ORANGE	Why not. You are improvising already, but you keep looking down. It is creating a barrier between the tourists and yourself. It might make you freer
SAMUEL	No I need to hold my script.
ORANGE	Just – just bring it!
SAMUEL	Orange /
	She grabs it from his hand, and stuffs it away. This is a terrible moment for SAMUEL. *Why would she do this?*
ORANGE	It's gone
SAMUEL	Why would you do that
ORANGE	Just be free, talk freely…
	Julie does it without the script.
SAMUEL	(*Panicking.*) It had all my notes on it, my – my –
	I'll forget what to say
	Only qualified tour guides should touch the…

ORANGE   You've done this many many times Samuel!
            You know what to say

LETTY   Samuel! Sorry, questions!

            How did you get into all of this? And how old
            are you today?

SAMUEL   Oh, um, ah I – I am not a hundred per cent
            sure of my exact age.

LETTY   Huh.

SAMUEL   Yes.

LETTY   But how would that work? Wouldn't your
            family – your parents know?

SAMUEL   No! I mean… I know it is my birthday, but
            yes, I lost track. It is a strange story, when
            I was small there were some years I was

            alone, around here… not for long, they
            always came back… but yes – and I… I…

            I am talking too much –

            Something shifts within him.

            (*Sharply*.) Please, do you have any questions
            about the castle – and Orange, please give me
            back my script!

            ORANGE *shakes her head.*

LETTY   What do they think about you doing this job?

SAMUEL   Who madam.

LETTY   Your family. Or friends… if you –

SAMUEL   Oh – um – (*To* ORANGE.) please, my script –
            I – I am forgetting the next part. My family –
            um, friends! Yes, they are all very proud,
            thank you.

            My mother says she is very proud of me.
            Every day. She sends me a message that says
            'good luck with the tours'.

            Ha.

ORANGE	I thought –
SAMUEL	Huh
	Oh
	oh, um, no
	No – Orange, shh
ORANGE	But –
SAMUEL	She sends me a message every day that says…
LETTY	Sorry am I asking too much
ORANGE	No no, you can ask anything you want – you want an authentic tour you will get one.
	I've got this Samuel, this way. To the condemned chamber!
	Samuel go on.

Trev and Letty are Locked in the Condemned Chamber

A highlight of the tour.

SAMUEL	Okay, um – so – this way please.
	The condemned chamber is the place where the rebellious ones were imprisoned to die.
	The resistance fighters. They were made an example of.
	It is our custom here, to give you an experience of their final moments.
	Please
	Enter in here.
TREV	Errrrmmm are you sure –

> TREV *and* LETTY *are led into the*
> *condemned chamber, and the door is closed.*

ORANGE   Samuel

SAMUEL   …Yes

ORANGE   You know you are my best friend here. My
            work husband in the castle.

SAMUEL   No. What do you want from me?

ORANGE   I have a surprise for you. I will reveal it in the
            governor's room

SAMUEL   No Orange no – I said, don't do that. It's bad
            luck, I don't want anything.

            Give me back my script –

ORANGE   Come on! You will like it

SAMUEL   In the governor's room, no – no that isn't
            appropriate –

            Beat.

            Orange. You know, when you asked me if
            I wanted to hurt the tourists…

ORANGE   That was a joke Samuel

SAMUEL   Yes, I know. I would never want to do
            anything – but…

            Ah

            Today the tourists have been getting to me.

            Maybe it is because I woke up in a strange
            mood. These two, for example. I don't know
            why. Ah. But I have been looking at them and
            imagining…

            He slowly gestures his hands around their
            necks.

            ORANGE *looks at* SAMUEL.

ORANGE   Oh.

SAMUEL	And just – I would just
	He keeps going. Transformed, for a moment.
	A prolonged silence. They both imagine this.
ORANGE	Samuel shhhh – they are talking.
SAMUEL	Forget what I said –
ORANGE	I cannot.
	ORANGE *and* SAMUEL *start to eavesdrop outside the condemned chamber.*
	TREV *and* LETTY *are in the condemned chamber. There is a silence as* LETTY *really tries to take it all in.* TREV *watches her.*
TREV	You alright?
LETTY	Yeah. Just weird isn't it.
TREV	…it was your idea.
LETTY	Sorry?
TREV	Nothing. Nothing.
LETTY	No, say it.
TREV	It was just a – never mind.
	I just said.
	That this was your idea.
LETTY	Right.
	Well yeah, you've made it really clear that this was my idea.
	TREV *is on his phone.*
	Why are you still on your phone!!
TREV	No reception down here – I'm just trying to…
LETTY	Just focus for once!!
	She focuses. She shivers.

TREV   Okay okay.

                You cold?

LETTY   Yeah.

                It's cold in here.

TREV   Want me to warm you up?

                LETTY *laughs for a quick moment, then grimaces.*

                Ahh come on.

LETTY   What are you on? No seriously. Are you trying to be funny – this is – I know you don't wanna be here but I just thought you'd want to be here for me. At least.

TREV   I know. I was just saying – one last time – that I don't think that being locked in the condemned chamber of Cape Coast Castle by a man called Samuel was something I saw for myself on my holiday, to be honest.

SAMUEL   (*Outside.*) Oh.

ORANGE   (*Outside.*) Okay he needs to stop saying that.

SAMUEL   (*Outside.*) Shh.

                LETTY *says nothing.*

TREV   Sorry. It's true.

                LETTY *stays silent.*

                And.

LETTY   And what.

TREV   Did you ever think this through?

LETTY   Think what.

TREV   About what I want.

LETTY   About what you want?

Yes. I do think about what you want all the time.

All of the time. This entire holiday has been about you, until now. We've done it all. Did I want to go to that club until four a.m.?

TREV   You had a great time.

ORANGE   (*Outside*.) Eyyy.

TREV   Don't say you didn't have a good time.

LETTY   Yes okay I had a good time but no that isn't the point. Did I want to spend all of that time with your five cousins? No. But I did. Because I think about you, all the time, what you want to do, and now I've asked for your attention or your support for one hour. One hour Trev – to stand with me, to support me through this – because, I don't know, I want to be here. Yeah. I want to be fucking locked up in here, because I want to feel it. What they might have felt I want to be here, to close the circle. The amount of money I've put in to do this — the amount of time...

One hour – I asked for one hour

SAMUEL *is nodding, like, 'That is fair.'*

TREV   Yeah I know babe. I know.

You wanna get out of here?

LETTY *is silent. She nods. They exit the courtyard and* ORANGE *and* SAMUEL *quickly scatter.*

Look I'm sorry.

LETTY   Yeah.

TREV   But you know like.

A long pause.

LETTY	What?
TREV	Nah nah. You need to get through this. One hour. I'm on it. Condemned chamber. I got you.
LETTY	No – go on. Say something. Come on
TREV	No no.
LETTY	You obviously have more to say.
TREV	Nope.
LETTY	Why open your mouth unless you're gonna use it?
TREV	Yep. Okay. Well. Well it's like, hello. This is the first time you have felt

Black,

right?

Pause.

ORANGE *and* SAMUEL *look at each other from the corner, like, 'Wooooooow'.*

No, but seriously. When you're in like, school, you see images of like this place, fucking locked-up, slaves… what are you seeing. Visualise it.

cos I actually see

myself in here.

LETTY	And I don't?
TREV	It's a bit different isn't it.

It's a little bit different.

LETTY	What are you trying to say.

The number of times I've been – been crying –

TREV	Yep.
LETTY	So I don't belong here. Because I'm not Black. I'm white. White English.
	I am a white English woman visiting Cape Coast Castle.
	That's me.
TREV	I'm just saying it's not the same.
LETTY	I shouldn't be here.
TREV	I'm just saying it's not the same.
LETTY	So I shouldn't feel something here?
TREV	I'm just saying it's not the same.
LETTY	And why isn't it the same?
TREV	Because it's not the same.
LETTY	And why isn't the same?
TREV	Because it's not the same.
LETTY	And why is it not the same?
ORANGE	(*Mouths.*) Answer her!!!
TREV	Because you've had a different experience than me, right.
LETTY	Right. What is this. A competition?
	Neither of us have had this experience.
TREV	No – but – you don't *see* yourself in here. Right. When was the last time you – like when you saw fucking *Roots*, or any slavery film – anyone who looks like you, they are in the house. Chilling.
LETTY	Wow. We are in an actual slave castle, and your reference is *Roots*?
TREV	It's true!
	Letty, why would I wanna come here. I didn't want to come home to do this. The fact you

wanna be here, that you're getting something from this – nah. Not trying to see myself here. Look at me. You see how it is. You know. And I get it – I get it – you're trying to connect, with, with half of yourself, not the white half, the other half – but this is the whole me. In here. Locked in here. For fuck's sake. You put me in here. Now what do you want me to do?

LETTY   You're not listening to me. I didn't want you to –

TREV   Nah I get it. Trust me, I've listened to you non-stop. I get it.

LETTY   …

TREV   I dunno… if we're gonna do anything

If we're gonna have kids –

LETTY   I'd want them to know everything.

TREV   Well I wouldn't raise them like what you've had –

LETTY   You don't get it.

TREV   That's what I'm saying to you! I don't.

Cos I'm just trying to have a nice time – with you, in the sun, for once

LETTY *is quiet.*

Look at me

No look at me

Listen to me

I wanna talk about different things

LETTY   I'm trying to look at you. This place – I don't know why but I had a feeling that this place would change something. Just settle me a bit. A pilgrimage like, one of those things.

Beat.

	If I want to be here
	To belong here
	I can.
	You have it – you have it all already –
TREV	I really do not.
	I really really do not.
LETTY	Where's Orange? Where is she?

Suddenly – almost too suddenly:

ORANGE	I am here miss – I am coming!
LETTY	Thanks. Okay. Can you show me where the bathroom is, I need to go –
ORANGE	Of course of course. This way.

They go off, leaving TREV *alone.*

After a moment, SAMUEL *approaches him.*

SAMUEL	Is everything okay sir.
TREV	What – Sam, you scared me there.
	Do you know what. No. Things are not okay.
SAMUEL	Oh okay. I am sorry to hear it.
TREV	Did you not just hear all that.
SAMUEL	Oh no sir. I heard nothing.

Pause.

	Would you like me to do anything?
TREV	Nah nah. Nah. You're good. Just – just stay there. Leave them to it.
SAMUEL	Okay.

They sit together in a silence.

TREV	Fuck this man.
SAMUEL	Oh.
	Miss Letty?

TREV   Yeah. Letty.

              I was just asking, why would she bring me
              here.

SAMUEL   Many people find something they need from
              this place.

TREV   This is the place for that? Really? No offence.

SAMUEL   Ah.

              I try my best to give the people what they
              need. It is not easy.

TREV   And how can you do it? Every day? In a place
              like this? Isn't that fucking you up?

              *SAMUEL ponders the question for a long
              time.*

              He doesn't respond.

              I should talk to her. Properly.

SAMUEL   Yes.

TREV   You got anyone? Been in love?

              This shakes SAMUEL. *More than he realises.*

SAMUEL   Ah! Me?! No. No no no no no. I am too busy
              working on my profession and

              thinking of

              God.

TREV   Ahhhh

              Fair fair fair.

              Well I'm about to fuck up what I've got. I'm
              gonna take an interest.

              ORANGE *and* LETTY *appear.*

ORANGE   Helloooo you two, you are having a big chat
              no. Please, are you ready for the secret

governor's residence? I will get my surprise and meet you there!

TREV   Okay okay. You alright Letty?

LETTY *bristles, shrugs*.

Alright let's do it.

To the Governor's Room

SAMUEL, TREV *and* LETTY *arrive in the governor's residence.* SAMUEL *seems a little out of sorts.*

SAMUEL   Okay. Welcome everybody to the governor's residence. We do not normally come in here. Please mind your heads. This is where the British would conduct their affairs.

TREV   What was the name of the person you were telling me about Letty the other day, the last governor? George, was it?

SAMUEL   Oh, yes. Yes. It was George Maclean, the final governor of this castle.

TREV   Right, right right.

(*To* LETTY.) Can we talk – I'm sorry…

LETTY *ignores him*.

LETTY   Go on Samuel.

He tries to get back into tour mode.

It is beautiful in here. Yes, truly beautiful. Very cool.

This is where the British

of course the British

well, they did like it here

This is where they managed the castle. It is
where they would pray, where they would write
their letters. It is where I think about Governor
George Maclean and his lover Letitia.

I think about them up here

together,

them writing their letters to England, letters of
the heart...

and if you turn to your right please, you can
look out of this window

see the sea, see the sea. The people who
didn't make it

Beat.

please, if you turn to the floor

if you look underneath the wooden floorboards

you can see the outlines of Male Dungeon
No. 5.

yes.

*He loses himself in distraction. Starts
speeding up.*

there it is.

so imagine it. George writing letters up here

because he is the governor to his lover Letitia

and he is conducting his affairs, the affairs of
the state

and below his feet

are my people.

He looks to LETTY.

Do you have any questions? About how the
British lived here. Rested here.

He loses himself in distraction.

LETTY
...where's all the –

TREV
Where's all the stuff? Yeah – is that what you were gonna say? The furniture, why's it so empty?

LETTY *looks at* TREV *like, 'What?'*

SAMUEL
Oh yes, no, you won't be able to see any of the original items of the British. They took it all away. Destruction of evidence. Destruction of a way of life. But we still do have a sense of what they did up here, whilst of course horrors took place below.

LETTY
Wow.

TREV
It's a lot.

Shall we get a photo Letty?

I know how much this means to you.

LETTY
Huh – no I don't think...

TREV
Yeah – just – something to remember us – you – being here, you know.

SAMUEL
Oh we don't usually take photos up in this – we are not supposed to be

TREV *takes the photo anyway.*

LETTY
Trev!

I'm so sorry Samuel –

SAMUEL
Okay back to the tour at hand. This is where George would write love letters to Letitia.

LETTY
...before we get back to it, I wanted to say. I'm sorry about your mother. I didn't realise when I said earlier about your family... I shouldn't have assumed anything. Orange told me.

SAMUEL
I am sorry?

LETTY
My mum passed, before I really knew her. Not got many memories of her. She would've – I can imagine that she would've loved to have

come here too. At least you knew yours, before she left – I guess you have memories?

SAMUEL   Oh no – no no no, not memories, no, she is – she did not leave me, no, she is just, she is on a trip. She will be – back soon – yes…

Beat.

I need my script? I have forgotten the next…

A moment.

TREV *is on his phone again.*

LETTY   Can you get off your phone please!

TREV   Wait! I've had an idea.

LETTY   Sorry Samuel. Go on.

SAMUEL   I must say it – it

angers me – the way the British

SAMUEL *is trying to regain control, but it is slipping away.*

A moment. It passes.

TREV   Okayyy done. Sorry Samuel, do you mind if I take a moment?

SAMUEL *nods.*

(*To* LETTY.) I've written you something.

LETTY   What are you doing?

TREV   A quick letter, like George and Letitia

LETTY   I'm not sure that's the point…

TREV   Just give me one second

Alright

Let's go

'Letty
You Are The Apple Of My Eye
When Ever I See You
There's Nothing But Clear Skies
When I'm With You Time Never Flies
You're My Beyoncé
We Feel Like '03 Bonnie And Clyde
You Are The Sugar To My Tea
The Butter To My Bread
I Love You All Around Yearly
Yours Sincerely,
Trev'

LETTY   You're so stupid.

TREV   I'm trying, aren't I

LETTY   Mmm.

You are quite sweet

No. We need to focus –

I am so sorry, you were saying saying
Samuel? This was their bedroom, right?

Where did they used to sleep?

SAMUEL   Oh. Oh yes –

He realises that TREV *and* LETTY *aren't
really listening, as they are increasingly
focused on each other.*

Perhaps the real question is:

– *how* could they sleep. Whilst knowing what
took place beneath their floorboards?

The – the bed would have been over there.
Where Mr Trev is.

LETTY   I wish I could've seen it.

TREV   Let's imagine it! Fuck the British, taking all
of their stuff with them – come on Letty, let's
go on the bed. Take back the bed.

LETTY	This is too much. You're still not taking it seriously.
TREV	I am I am. We gotta experience this. All of it.
LETTY	I'm –
TREV	Look, I'm trying to get into it. I'm sorry for what I said.
LETTY	I know.
	I'm sorry too. For making you /
TREV	Forget it. Let's make the most of it now. Come on. We should be able to rest on the actual bed the British slept on.
SAMUEL	They took the bed with them. In around 1889.
	I would also like to see the bed
	I would also like to lie on the bed
	Beat.
	They start to go towards the location of the missing bed.
TREV	We're just going to have a little lie-down like George and Letitia... come on Letts, this is your one and only chance.
LETTY	Okayyyy –
	Something strange happens as LETTY *settles into the non-existent bed.*
	It is almost like they are falling into a sleep-like state, an unreal place.
	you know it does feel good...
	it's so comfortable... just to know where
	those savages –
	the British – slept...
SAMUEL	Oh, madam, sir, please – I think it is bad luck to do this

TREV   Nah we gotta feel the bed. How could they do
                this, sleeping soundly. Fuck that.

                *The longer they stay on 'the bed', the more it
                seems to pull them into a dreamlike frenzy.
                Meanwhile,* SAMUEL *tries to say serious,
                and to keep things in the present. The
                following from* LETTY *and* TREV *becomes
                increasingly spoken in a heightened British
                1800s voice.*

LETTY   Yesssss. Just to know that this is where those

                savages

                the history of this place.

                They look at him.

SAMUEL   Please –

                this is where…

TREV   Where what, Samuel?

SAMUEL   This is where

LETTY   George and Letitia.

SAMUEL   This is where

                the savages

                slept

LETTY   that's what I just said

TREV   Letters of the heart

SAMUEL   no

                yes, I mean – this is where the

                the the the

                sleep

                Orange – oh that girl, my script – where are
                you –

LETTY   Samuel come and join me! Come on – you
               said you want to feel it too, feel where they
               slept, what they did – let's do something
               different! I want a personalised tour, you said
               that was possible didn't you?

               *They start slipping more and more into the
               past, and only focusing on each other.*

TREV   Comfortable sleep Letts? Would you like me
               to warm you up?

LETTY   Ohhh you are bad! It was just perfect. And
               now just another day waking up at this castle!

TREV   Castle!

LETTY   It is just so tiring – so tiring – administrating
               this damned place.

SAMUEL   Madam

TREV   Are you hot? I'm hot too

LETTY   So hot! Could do with a glass of water – what
               a terrible state I'm in!

TREV   Lots to do, lots to do, letters to write – affairs
               of the mind and the heart!

LETTY   My gosh I feel like I will die out here! I don't
               like it here Georgie! It doesn't feel quite
               right!

SAMUEL   Please – please, stop – what is happening –
               I do not think –

               *Slowly they look up and it feels as if they have
               just seen* SAMUEL *for the first time. It is like
               a lucid dream. The room feels like it has
               tilted.*

               Slowly, TREV *and* LETTY *appear to
               transform before* SAMUEL*'s eyes into
               George Maclean (former governor of the
               castle) and his lover Letitia.*

TREV/GEORGE What are you doing up here?

SAMUEL   Um – I am sorry – I am working – Trev…?

TREV/GEORGE Letitia! Letitia! There's a man in our
                        bedroom!

LETTY/LETITIA   Oh my goodness!

                        There's a man in our bedroom

TREV/GEORGE You shouldn't be up here, stay away

                        Stay away – be careful

                        This room – this room isn't for you

                        What's your number? How did you get up
                        here

LETTY/LETITIA   George!!

TREV/GEORGE Go! Now!

SAMUEL   I work here sir – I am touring – please

TREV/GEORGE Get out! You will be punished for this!

LETTY/LETITIA   I'm scared. I should have never come here
                        George.

SAMUEL   Wake up! Are you awake?

TREV/GEORGE They won't hurt you

                        I wouldn't let that – that happen

                        Stay back –

SAMUEL   Trev, are you in there? Trev? Letty…?

TREV/GEORGE Get out. Get out, get out, get out, get out!!!!!
                        Or else!

SAMUEL   I am – I am – I am going –

                        SAMUEL *tries to leave, he trips, he panics.*

                        ORANGE *enters with a cake.* TREV *and*
                        LETTY *reset – maybe they aren't even on the*

*bed any more, they seem to have no
recollection of what has just happened.*

ORANGE   Surpriseeeeee. Eyyyyyy happy birthdayyyyyy
time everybody!!

Samuel you don't look well! I have cake!

*She clocks the strange atmosphere, but
marches on ahead anyway.* SAMUEL *blows
the candles but the cake slips from*
ORANGE*'s hands and falls.*

Beat.

(*To* SAMUEL.) Is everyone okay here? Why
the sad face Samuel? It has been a long day,
we've only got one stop left. I can take it over
from here Samuel, if you are tired. Shall we
toast?

LETTY   Yes, yes I think we should. To… to…
Samuel!

TREV   To Samuel

ALL   To Samuel!

SAMUEL just looks at them.

ORANGE   And Happy Year of Return everyone!!!

SAMUEL   No! Stop! Hello everyone

you are welcome

to my eleventh – eleventh – tour of the

day.

reset reset reset

He looks at TREV *and* LETTY. *Why are they
still there?*

*Why can't he reset to the next tour???? The
next day???*

??????

LETTY	Why is he saying that? What did he say before?
	SAMUEL *looks at* TREV, *says nothing, wonders why he can't speak right now.*
TREV	(*To* SAMUEL.) Can we talk? Can we –
SAMUEL	Next tour!
TREV	You got anyone?
SAMUEL	Next tour!
TREV	Come on. Just tell me – come on! You have to live.
LETTY	Samuel…
	like my cousin! Samuel – my cousin!!!
SAMUEL	Next room please
	Next tourists please
	Tour is over tour is over – they need to go, they are not safe!
ORANGE	To the Door of No Return! Let's gooooo!!
	SAMUEL *looks at his watch, but time isn't speeding on, why is he still in this tour???*
SAMUEL	Did you see what happened? What just happened – they – they…
	There's a feeling of chaos. SAMUEL *feels increasingly trapped and confused.*
	Orange please… this is too much…
ORANGE	Door of No Return!!! Let's go!!!
	ORANGE *exits with* TREV *and* LETTY.

The Door of No Return

ORANGE	Okay! We are here everybody, at the Door of No Return. Samuel, something is not right, do you want to speak?
SAMUEL	Oh no, no Orange – I am okay. But you go.
ORANGE	Thank you.

I am aware that this has been a difficult tour, with many emotions. But we are so happy that you have made it to this point. For you Letty, this may have been the last place your ancestors stood before they were put onto the ships. Ships with names like *Sally*, names like *Star*. For real. That was the last moment they saw Ghana, or African soil. The last moment they were truly themselves.

But us here – you there – are the children of the survivors. Those who made it to other shores. And now, you can pass through and stand where they stood.

But this time, you will return.

TREV, *by this point, has won over* LETTY. ORANGE *ushers them to start going towards the door.*

SAMUEL	Wait.
ORANGE	What is it, Samuel?
SAMUEL	They should not go through.
ORANGE	Eh?
SAMUEL	You both – you should not go through. I do not think it is safe. You do not know what just happened.
ORANGE	What do you mean, not safe?
SAMUEL	We cannot trust… we cannot guarantee that they will return.

LETTY	It's what I've wanted to do, since I heard about this place.
TREV	Yeah come on, it'll be alright Sam – like we spoke about, closing the circle.
SAMUEL	Yes – yes, but no. I have a bad feeling. Something is going wrong with me, with the castle. Um. A strange feeling. This tour. I never do more than my ten. That's what I always say. It is our duty – as tour guides – to make sure that each guest returns. Because many – many did not.
ORANGE	It is just a castle. It is just a door Samuel.
SAMUEL	It is more than a door! Orange... ah! You don't know. If you aren't careful...
	You will stay here – You will stay here Orange, you will stay here with me, in the ticketing booth assisting me and there is nowhere else you can go, you will always be doing that!
ORANGE	No, that's you Samuel, that's not me. One day I'm gonna be out of here, it's not good for our blossoming friendship
	You will see me on TV!
	It is true!
	Do you ever leave the castle Samuel?
SAMUEL	I leave! We walk out together every day –
ORANGE	No we don't
	We've never left together
TREV	We're gonna go through the door Samuel.
SAMUEL	No – no I don't – please –
LETTY	I'm sorry Samuel, this is something that I need to do for myself.
	Beat.

SAMUEL starts to panic.

She slowly starts to walk through the door.

TREV   How does it feel?

LETTY   I feel

        I feel

        I think I feel nothing.

TREV   Right.

LETTY   Maybe... maybe we got the wrong castle?

        I – I – I don't think they were taken from
        here, maybe we could look for another castle?

TREV   Letty?

LETTY   No

        No you're right

        Not another castle, we just need to try

        all the castles

        I think I'll know it when I find the right castle

TREV   Or maybe we should go home?

LETTY   Home?

TREV   Yeah.

LETTY   But I think I'll know it when I'm in the right
        one, this isn't the right one

        I know it now, they weren't in this one

TREV   We might not find them in any of the castles

LETTY   We try one more?

        You wouldn't have to come in with me

        She looks panicked.

        She is never going to find the right castle.

She remains in the frame of the door.

TREV   …or we could just leave it

LETTY   Leave it?

TREV   Would you want to

            …forget it

LETTY   No say it

TREV   Would you want to

            would you want to just be with me?

            We could, you know

            just go home.

LETTY   Huh.

TREV   I wanna be with you

            A long pause.

LETTY   I think I'd like that.

            Would she?

            SAMUEL *is watching in pain.*

TREV   Let's go through together.

LETTY   Okay.

            TREV *and* LETTY *start to go through the
            door.*

ORANGE   I am going through with them.

SAMUEL   Please. Stay with me.

            I feel something will happen, I will do
            something –

ORANGE   Samuel, you don't look well, I am just taking
            them through.

            *She joins them. As they walk through the door
            to the beach,* SAMUEL *sits alone.*

SAMUEL   You will not come back.

Beat.

SAMUEL *waits.*

Waits.

Then ORANGE *returns.*

They are gone?

ORANGE   Yes.

Samuel, what is going on?

SAMUEL   Sometimes I see – I see –

sometimes I feel

He speeds up.

that I am in fact more than fine, I am happy here!

Of course this place is hard. But I do it for all of you. I want you to have a good time, to remember your experience, to feel at home.

Resets.

Sometimes I see – I see –

sometimes I feel

like – like I want

to get my hands on all of them.

yes.

I will say 'Do you feel at home?'

Beat.

I will say 'I am your brother!

It is me!'

He laughs. Stops.

Whilst I... I...

yes.

I don't know why I see this in my sleep.

Do you know why…

I see them all in my sleep

I see…

in my sleep…

Beat.

ORANGE   The castle – you don't look…

You can't do this job like this…

SAMUEL   You will become a serious… too…

ORANGE   No.

SAMUEL   I can't leave here – it is the Year of Return, she might be…

she might be returning

Beat.

you said:

and I said:

and then I was gone

and – and – I couldn't find

couldn't find the place again

I kept walking and I

she

I don't

I thought she might return this year

One of the tourists might

might have information

'Crucial intel!'

might know

might have been sent to tell me, where to find her

you know

Orange do you know, can you help me find her?

Maybe?

ORANGE   I can't do that Samuel

Beat.

she isn't

sometimes they just…

go.

Beat.

I'll take it from here.

ORANGE *leaves*.

SAMUEL *looks up at us all*.

Hello.

I am Samuel.

You are welcome to

my – my tour of the day, and I am

looking forward to

getting to know you

inside and over the next hour.

I love my work.

(*Rest*.)

Full of

LIFE

?

?????

You want me to be

full of life?????

Orange. Orange?

??

My...

great-great-great-grand–

was taken down to the coast

left the coast

I forget

something about the coast

he was –

um, he

was found!

he found his people again

and sometimes, well

sometimes I think I am that

I am that man

Yes

Hm. That man.

waiting for his people to come

I thought

I thought it might happen this year

Year of Return!

I thought it might be tonight

I don't know

my mother used to tell me this story, I – I

I was always sure that it might be me

He wakes up from his reverie. Realises that nobody is really hearing him.

Pause. This moment should feel like he is going off-script...

Oh. Sorry. I think I see now. Yes.

I want to be alone.

My mother always says – always says, 'good luck with your tour', every day.

Hallo! HalloooooooooooOoooooooooo. Dry. Dry Samuel. Wearisome Samuel.

Ah.

Am letting go.

I think I might   everyone, I...   I might

I might –

just

yes.

I will

stop.   Orange is right,   I will, I think –

it is time to take a break...

He leaves.

ACT THREE. MORNING

Orange Stands in for Samuel and She's Great

Good morning. Next day. The air is soft. The sea is relaxed.
ORANGE gets ready. She takes a deep breath in. And she
delivers a tour. She is utterly brilliant and strikes the balance
perfectly. A natural public speaker.

ORANGE   Hello everybody and

Happy Year of Return.

You are welcome to

my first tour of the day.

I am
looking forward to
getting to know you
all of you
over the next hour or so.

My name is Orange.

(Rest.)

How does it feel?

(Rest.)

To be here today.

(Rest.)

Anybody?

Anybody?

End of play.

A Nick Hern Book

Samuel Takes a Break…in Male Dungeon No. 5 After a Long But Generally Successful Day of Tours first published in Great Britain in 2024 as a paperback original by Nick Hern Books Limited, The Glasshouse, 49a Goldhawk Road, London W12 8QP, in association with The Yard Theatre, London

Samuel Takes a Break…in Male Dungeon No. 5 After a Long But Generally Successful Day of Tours copyright © 2024 Rhianna Ilube

Rhianna Ilube has asserted her moral right to be identified as the author of this work

Cover image: photograph of Malick Bojang by Daniel Chan; concept by Kia Noakes

Designed and typeset by Nick Hern Books, London
Printed in the UK by Mimeo Ltd, Huntingdon, Cambridgeshire PE29 6XX

A CIP catalogue record for this book is available from the British Library

ISBN 978 1 83904 318 5

www.nickhernbooks.co.uk/environmental-policy

www.nickhernbooks.co.uk

facebook.com/nickhernbooks

twitter.com/nickhernbooks